The Resurrection Appearances of Our Lord

The Resurrection Appearances of Our Lord

by

Edgar Dowse

AVON BOOKS
1 DOVEDALE STUDIOS
465 BATTERSEA PARK ROAD
LONDON SW11 4LR

Printed and bound in the U.K.

Avon Books

London

First Published 1996

ISBN 1 86033 981 6

To My Beautiful

Acknowledgement

The Author wishes to thank the Anglican Society for their invitation to deliver these lectures and Miss A. Dooley who very kindly typed them.

Contents

Preface

These six lectures are reproduced as they were first delivered during the Great Forty Days in 1992. I hope they will strengthen the faith of the ordinary Christian, for whom they are intended. I also hope they will confute any unbelievers who may happen to read them.

The importance of the Resurrection of Jesus Christ cannot be over-estimated. It is the greatest and most significant event in the history of the world, the event which establishes, once and for all, the truth of the Gospel and provides the one and only hope of the ultimate triumph of the purposes of God over evil. The fact that it is ignored by many people today is a measure of the obtuseness of modern secularism.

Christians have never ceased to proclaim that 'Jesus is alive!' and a few years ago a Christian publicist persuaded the Post Office to stamp this message on letters posted during the Easter season. A similar effort should be made again to tell the world that we have the truth!

It is very important that we should understand what the Resurrection means, and I have tried to make this clear in these lectures. It was not just an extraordinary event which happened to Jesus, an event to be studied in isolation from all other events. The Resurrection was the supreme example of the intervention of God in the affairs of this world. The Bible is about the God who speaks of acts, the God who reveals Himself in His 'mighty acts'. If we accept the Bible view of God, we need not be surprised that He has made Himself known in quite unexpected ways. Christmas, Good Friday, Easter Day and Pentecost represent the chief stages in God's action. I hope that what I have written will remind readers of the tremendous nature of the Resurrection of Jesus Christ as a fact. In this we rejoice 'with joy unspeakable and full of glory'.

Edgar Dowse

The Resurrection Appearances of Our Lord (Lecture 1)

The stories in the New Testament of the Resurrection Appearances of Our Lord are of supreme importance. In the first place, they confirm the evidence of the Empty Tomb. The fact that the tomb in which Our Lord's body was laid was found to be empty on the third day, the fact that the tomb was open and unguarded and that the grave clothes were found in the shape of the body, all point to an extraordinary and unexpected event and give meaning to the message of the angels to the women, "He is not here. He has risen." But belief in the resurrection, that God by a mighty act of power completely reversed all that the world had done by the rejection and crucifixion of Jesus, and showed Him to be alive and the conqueror of death; this conviction needed an additional reinforcement, a final crowning demonstration; and this was provided by the Resurrection Appearances.

In the second place, these Appearances were necessary in order to establish the identity of the risen Christ with the Jesus of Nazareth whom the disciples had known and loved. A mere series of events demonstrating the "livingness" of Jesus, to use the word of a former Bishop of Durham*, would not have been sufficient to remove all doubt. The disciples had

*David Jenkins

to be sure, otherwise they would have had no gospel to preach. The effect of the Appearances may be seen in the breathless exclamation of Mary Magdalene, “I have seen The Lord!” In St John’s “It is The Lord!” and in the confession of St Thomas “My lord and my God.”

There can be no doubt about the fundamental importance of the Resurrection. Hebrews, 13^{20} speaks of the God “Who brought back from the dead Our Lord Jesus.” Romans, 1^{4} refers to Jesus Christ “Who through the Spirit of Holiness was declared with power to be the Son of God by His resurrection from the dead.” In Romans, $6,^{9\text{-}11}$ the new life of the Christian is linked with the life of the Risen Christ: “For we know that since Christ was raised from the dead, He cannot die again; death no longer has mastery over Him. The death He died He died to sin once for all; but the life He lives, He lives to God. In the same way, count yourselves dead to sin but alive to God in Christ Jesus.” In 1 Peter, $1^{3\text{-}4}$ we have an outburst of joy: “Praise be to the God and Father of Our Lord Jesus Christ! In His great mercy He has given us new birth to a living hope through the resurrection of Jesus Christ from the dead, and into an inheritance that can never perish, spoil or fade - kept in heaven for you! The words APHTHARTON KAI AMIANTON KAI AMARANTON sound a shout of triumph!

The crucifixion of Jesus is regarded in the New Testament as having been brought about by evil spiritual powers, the "spiritual forces of evil in the heavenly realms," against which, according to Ephesians, 6^{12} the Christian has to fight. St Paul, in 1 Corinthians, 2^{8} refers to the "rulers of this age" (ARCHONTES TOU AIONOS TOUTOU), who crucified the Lord of Glory. When He was arrested, Jesus said "This is your hour, and the hour of darkness" (HE EXOUSIA TOU SKOTOUS). He had already spoken of "the prince of this world" who "has no hold on me". The Cross itself was a victory in which "Having disarmed the powers and authorities, He made a public Spectacle of them, triumphing over them by the cross" (Colossians, 2^{15}). From these references it is clear that the earliest Christians saw the death of Jesus as the supreme effort of the "powers and authorities of the present evil age" to gain control, to assert their dominion, and consequently they saw the resurrection as the greatest possible victory. Jesus had been vindicated by God "Who exerted His mighty strength when He raised Jesus from the dead and seated Him at His right hand in the heavenly realms, far above all rule and authority, power and dominion, and every title that can be given." (Ephesians $1^{19\text{-}21}$). Archbishop Ramsay reminded us that we should never think of the cross without the resurrection or the resurrection without the cross. This was certainly the attitude of the Church in the New Testament period.

There is a passion, a joy, a conviction, a certainty in the New Testament documents which impinges on the mind of anyone who studies them seriously. J. B. Phillips[1] describes the impression which the Gospels made on him as a translator: 'Here, through the incomplete and sometimes almost naive records, one is in contact with something so tremendous in its significance that at first the mind cannot grasp it, but only, as it were, gasps incredulously. Previously one had accepted the teaching of the Church's Creeds - that Jesus was both Man and God, and to say one believed in the "Incarnation" would not raise an eyebrow anywhere. But now from first hand acquaintance with these early documents the truth sweeps in afresh, and the indescribable humility of God strikes one with overwhelming awe. This little sphere on which we live, move and have our being is, in fact, a Visited Planet. The Creator of the vast universe, about whose nature we could at the most make intelligent guesses, slipped quietly into the stream of human life in the only way in which that could be possible - by becoming a human being. This is the truth that pulses and vibrates behind the steady prose of Matthew, Mark and Luke and shines through the more poetic work of John.'

If the story of Jesus had ended with His death, the four Gospels would never have been written. If any memory of Him had remained it would have been the memory of a pathetic failure. Crucifixion was not only a most painful form of execution (*Crudelissimum taeterimmumque supplicium*, said Cicero), it was also a disgraceful death, the death of the rebel and the slave. The enemies of Jesus knew what they were about when they shouted "Crucify". Their object was not merely to destroy Jesus but to discredit Him. Nothing is more astonishing than the attitude of the earliest Christians to the Cross. To people of the first century the cross was a terrible instrument of torture, a symbol of horror. Yet here is St Paul saying 'May I never boast except in the cross of Our Lord Jesus Christ, through which the world has been crucified to me, and I to the world.' Such language would have been regarded as indecent, repulsive and utterly unintelligible unless something tremendous had happened which had given an entirely new meaning to the death of Jesus and had changed the greatest tragedy into the greatest triumph. That transformation had been brought about by the resurrection. It could not possibly have been effected by anything else.

The resurrection is a great deal more than a "happy ending" to a story. It is the source of that presence of the living Christ which is the daily experience of the Christian and the secret of the joyful worship of the Church. THANATO THANATON PATESAS, says the ancient liturgy and this is repeated in the Prayer Book on Easter Day: "Who by

His death hath destroyed death, and by His rising to life again hath restored to us everlasting life." All down the Christian centuries Christians have rejoiced in what St Paul called "the power of His resurrection". Here is the testimony of the great St Athanasius[2] in the fourth century: "When a man is dead he can exert no power, his influence lasts to the grave and then ceases. Actions and power over men belong to the living only. Then let him who will, see, and judge from what his eyes behold. For the Saviour is working great things among men. Every day He is invisibly persuading a great multitude from every quarter, both Greeks and foreigners to come over to His faith and to obey His teaching. Will anyone still be in doubt whether the resurrection has been accomplished by the Saviour, and whether Christ be alive, or rather be Himself the life? ... Or how, if He be not active (for that is the peculiarity of the dead) does He restrain from their activity those who are active and living, so that the impure man is no longer impure, the homicide slays no more, the unrighteous is no longer covetous, the profane is henceforth religious? ... This is not the work of the dead, but of the living, and especially of God."

The subject of these lectures is the Resurrection appearances, but these cannot be studied without preliminary consideration of the significance of the resurrection itself and so a lengthy introduction has been necessary. The Appearances may be listed as follows: the first, to Mary Magdalene on the morning of the Easter Day; the second to the women who were returning from the tomb; the third to St Peter; the fourth to the two disciples who walked to Emmaus; the fifth to the disciples and others on the evening of the Easter Day; the sixth to the disciples a week later; the seventh to a few disciples beside the Lake of Galilee; the eighth to the Apostles and some five hundred followers; the ninth to St James; the tenth to the disciples who were present at the Ascension. It will also be necessary to say something about the Appearance to St Paul on the road to Damascus and those to St Stephen at his death and to St John the author of the Book of Revelation. Some of the Appearances took place on the first Easter Day and others during the period known as the Great Forty Days. Some Appearances took place in Jerusalem or its neighbourhood and others elsewhere. Attempts have been made to drive a wedge between the Jerusalem and Galilee Appearances, but everything becomes clear if we assume that the disciples remained in Jerusalem for the first week and then reassembled in Galilee. Towards the end of the forty days they returned to Jerusalem, in accordance with their Lord's instructions. This solution to the problem was suggested by H. Latham in his books *Pastor Pastorum* and *The Risen Master*.

It is frequently said that the evidence for the resurrection depends on the Appearances alone. The story of the empty tomb is regarded as a late invention having no historical value. In reply it cannot be too strongly emphasised that the first disciples were Jews, and to a Jew resurrection could only mean one thing, namely, a physical resurrection. As Murray J. Harris[3] has written "Those who reject a physical resurrection are obliged to posit one of the following unconvincing hypotheses: that Jesus merely swooned on the cross and then recovered in the cool tomb; that the women visited the wrong tomb; that Jesus' body was stolen, either by His disciples or by His enemies; that His body was placed in a common grave or was burned on the rubbish heaps outside Jerusalem or was cremated by His disciples..." Dr Harris adds "It stretches credulity beyond the limit to believe that men were willing to suffer and die for what they knew to be a gigantic hoax and that the truth never slipped out, even to other followers of Jesus." Unlike the Greeks, the Jews did not find it easy to believe in the soul having an independent existence apart from the body. Oesterley and Robinson[4] say "To the Greek, man was essentially a spirit temporarily imprisoned in a body, and it was natural that when a body decayed, the liberated soul should continue to exist and to pursue its course. The Hebrew, on the other hand, thought of man as a body animated by a spirit, and when he developed a doctrine of immortality, it naturally took the form of a resurrection of the body." It was only when Jews were strongly influenced by Greek ideas that they thought of the soul as an independent essence, and there is no evidence of any such Greek influence upon the writers of the Gospels or the disciples. It follows that the empty tomb is the necessary presupposition of the resurrection appearances.

It has been said many times that the accounts of the events of the first Easter Day contradict one another and are irreconcilable. It can, however, be shown that they are complementary, and a recent convincing harmonisation has been set out by John Wenham in his book *Easter Enigma.* An early harmony of the four accounts is in the Diatessaron of Tatian, an English translation of which was published by T. and T. Clark in 1894. The tremendous importance of the Resurrection Appearances is stressed by Karl Barth[5], the greatest theologian of this century. He says "The Easter Story, Christ truly, corporeally risen, and as such appearing to His disciples, talking with them, acting in their midst - this is, of course, the recollection upon which all New Testament recollections hang, to which they are all related, for the sake of which there is a New Testament recollection at all."

In order to understand the events of the first Easter Day it is necessary to begin with Good Friday and to study carefully the records of the burial of Jesus. Jesus died at 3.00 in the afternoon. St John tells us that the Jews asked Pilate to order the crurifragium, the breaking of the legs, so that those crucified might die quickly from suffocation, and the bodies could be removed to prevent defilement of the Sabbath. The soldiers broke the legs of the two robbers but refrained from doing this to Jesus because He appeared to be dead. However, one of the soldiers pierced the side of Jesus with a spear and there was a sudden flow of blood and water from the wound. St John regards this incident as very significant. It fulfilled scriptural prophecies in Exodus 12^{46}, Numbers 9^{12}, Psalm 34^{20}, and Zechariah 12^{10}. St John emphasises in the strongest terms that he is speaking the truth. "The man who saw it has given testimony, and this testimony is true. He knows that he tells the truth, and he testifies so that you may believe." The spear thrust proved beyond any doubt that Jesus was already dead. At this point Joseph of Arimathea appears in the story. St John says "He was a disciple of Jesus, but secretly because he feared the Jews." St Matthew describes him as a rich man who had become a disciple of Jesus. St Mark adds that he was a prominent member of the Sanhedrin, and St Luke informs us that he was a good and upright man who had not voted for the condemnation of Jesus. Joseph determined to give the body of Jesus decent burial in a tomb which he had had cut out of the rock. He went boldly to Pilate (TOLMESAS says Mark) and asked for the body of Jesus. It is important to realise that there would have been some delay while Pilate gave orders to see whether Jesus was dead, and when at last permission was given there would have been very little time to complete the burial arrangements before sunset, when the Sabbath would begin. It was usual to dress a dead man in his own garment but the clothes of Jesus had been disposed of, so Joseph bought a SINDON in the market. This would have been a large linen cloth about 14 feet long and 3 feet wide. We are told that he wrapped the body in it. The word ENETULIXEN is from the rare verb ENTULISSEIN meaning to "wrap up". We must imagine the body of Jesus being laid in the SINDON which would then be passed over the head and back to the feet. The SINDON would be kept in place by what St John calls OTHONIA, linen bandages. St John tells us that Joseph was assisted by Nicodemus, who brought a large quantity of myrrh and aloes. This in solid or powdered form would be inserted in the folds of the OTHONIA. It was the custom to anoint a body before burial, but it is likely that this was not done on this occasion. The remark of Jesus in John 12[7] when Mary of Bethany anointed Him probably reflects the knowledge that His body was not, in fact, anointed. Joseph and Nicodemus then carried the body to the tomb and placed it on the ledge provided for a body. All this work was done so hurriedly that they almost forgot one important detail: it was the custom to tie a bandage around the face and under the chin. When Joseph and Nicodemus remembered this, there was no time to unwrap the body, so the face bandage, SOUDARION, was placed around the face on top of the SINDON. This was to prove important for it would be seen by Peter and John on the Easter morning. For the placing of a bandage around the face we notice the reference to Lazarus in John 11^{44}, KAI HE OPSIS AUTOU SOUDARIO PERIEDEDETO.

Some of the women, notably Mary Magdalene and "the other Mary", as she is called, watched the carrying of the body to the tomb and the closing of it with a large stone. They were not able to help for custom ruled that women must not interfere with men's work out of doors, but they went home and prepared "spices and perfumes" (AROMATA KAI MURA, as Luke says) and decided to return to the tomb as soon as possible on the Sunday morning. A question now arises: what did the women intend to do? Did they expect to unwrap the body and disturb the large quantity of myrrh and aloes which had already been placed around it? It is probable that the women had no clear idea as to what they would do. They were simply acting on a deep feminine instinct to "do something". In a terrible crisis, when all seems to be lost, men tend to collapse and do nothing. But women keep going, they do something. This is because women are built physically and mentally to care for children, and when you are in charge of children you cannot "give up". Life has to go on. It was therefore in response to this fundamental instinct that the women went to the tomb on the Easter morning.

Before we discuss the events of the Easter Day, it is necessary to notice the placing of a guard at the tomb which Matthew says took place on the Sabbath. We are told that the chief priests and the Pharisees went to Pilate and asked that the tomb should be guarded until the third day. Pilate's reply is ambiguous in Greek; "ECHETE KOUSTODIAN" could mean either "You have soldiers under your command, make use of them", or it could have been permission to ask for a guard of Roman soldiers. A. H. M'Neile favours the latter. John Wenham's[6] comment is instructive: "The story of the setting of the guard is one of the most extraordinary pieces of Christian apologetic ever written. As we have said, it bristles with improbabilities at every point: the Sabbath visit to the governor, the great earthquake, the flashing angel rolling back the stone, the reporting to the chief priests, the bribe to the soldiers to tell the tale that they were asleep on duty - everything invites, not belief, but incredulity. And how stupid, having introduced the useful apologetic idea of a closely guarded tomb, to give a handle to the opposition by even hinting that the guards did not do their job! It is a worthless piece of Christian apologetic at whatever date it was written, unless it happens to be undeniably true." What is certain is that when the women came to the tomb on the Easter morning it was open and unguarded and there was nothing to prevent the women from going inside. Matthew says that the first event of that day was a great earthquake and an angel appeared and rolled away the stone and sat on it. “His appearance was like lightning and his clothes were white as snow. The guards were so afraid of him that they shook and became like dead men.” It is clear that the soldiers ran away in a panic. Men whose courage is equal to any situation in battle will give way to fear in the presence of something which they regard as supernatural.

The women who arrived at the tomb soon after were Mary Magdalene, Mary Cleophas, Salome and Joanna. The name Mary, in the form Mariam, was very common among the Jews of the first century, partly in reference to Miriam the sister of Moses and partly out of sympathy for the Hasmonean princess Mariamne who had been murdered by King Herod. Mary Magdalene was from Magdala on the shore of the lake of Galilee. She is frequently identified with the woman of Luke 7^{36-50} who anointed Jesus. She is also identified with Mary of Bethany who anointed Jesus according to Matthew 26^{6-13}, Mark 14^{3-9}, John 12^{1-8}, cf 11^{17-32} and Luke 10^{28-42}. John Wenham accepts this identification, but it does seem that two different women are involved. Mary Magdalene is bold, impetuous and a natural leader; Mary of Bethany is quiet, meek and submissive. Luke tells us that seven demons had gone out of Mary Magdalene, an expression that probably means that she had experienced a moral and psychological, as well as a spiritual conversion. Of the other women, Mary Cleophas was the wife of Alphaeus, or Cleophas or Clopas, and the mother of four disciples of Jesus; Matthew, Thomas, James the Less and Simon. These relationships were worked out many years ago by Canon Peter Green in a little book called *Some Gospel Scenes and Characters*. Matthew, whose other name was Levi, is called the son of Alphaeus in Mark 2^{14}. Thomas must have had another name besides 'the twin', and the Acts of Thomas say it was Judas. He is always bracketed with Matthew which suggests that he was his brother. James 'the Less' or 'the Little' is said to be son of Alphaeus in Mark 3^{19}. The early writer Hegisippus refers to Simon son of Alphaeus whom it is reasonable to identify with Simon the Zealot. We should note that Salome was the sister of the Blessed Virgin Mary and the mother of the disciples James and John, and Joanna was the wife of Chuza, who is described in Luke 8^{2} as the EPITROPOS, or manager of the household of Herod Antipas. There may have been other women including Susanna, mentioned in Luke 8^{3}.

On approaching the tomb the women were surprised to see that the stone had been rolled away. Mary Magdalene, who had the kind of mind that could take in only one thing at a time, thought that tomb robbers had been at work, and without entering the tomb she ran back to tell Peter and John. The other women went into the tomb. They saw that the body of Jesus was not there but they did not examine the grave clothes which were lying in their place because they saw two angels who greeted them with a very plain statement: "He is not here for He is risen!" We can be quite sure that this is a true story, for anyone inventing it would have been unable to resist embellishing it at this point. We can see what imagination could do from the Apocryphal Gospel of Peter. Notice that Mark describes the angel who spoke to the women as a "young man dressed in a white robe", and this corresponds to the description of an angel in 2 Maccabees, 3[26,33] and Josephus ANT. 5[8.2]. The women came away from the tomb in a complex emotional state. They were puzzled, frightened, joyful, bewildered, all at the same time.

On hearing Mary Magdalene's news Peter and John ran to the tomb. John arrived first and looked into the tomb. He saw the grave clothes lying in the shape of the body. The SINDON was there, covered with the OTHONIA. The word used for John's 'seeing' is BLEPEI meaning 'he noticed'. When Peter arrived he did not hesitate, but in his usual impulsive way went straight into the tomb. Peter stared at the grave clothes, the word is THEOREI. The SOUDARION, which had been round the Lord's face, was lying there on top of the SINDON where it had been put on the outside. John's peculiar way of describing this is OU META TON OTHONION KEIMENON ALLA CHORIS ENTETULIGMENON EIS HENA TOPON. The NIV translation of this is 'Folded up by itself, separate from the linen'. The RSV has 'Not lying with the linen cloths but rolled up in a place by itself', which is better. The Greek is certainly unusual, but the Peshitto Syriac is helpful as it has CAD CARIQ which means 'like a round thing' for the Greek ENTETULIGMENON. It was the sight of this which made Peter stare. It made John realise that the Lord's body had passed out of the grave clothes. 'He saw and believed' it is said, and now the word EIDEN is used which means that he saw and understood.

Peter and John went away wondering and when they had gone Mary Magdalene returned alone. She stood at the entrance to the tomb weeping bitterly, for she could only think that someone had stolen the body. When she saw two angels in the tomb seated where the body had been, she was not impressed; and when they asked her 'Why are you crying?' it seemed a silly question, and she replied petulantly, 'They have taken my Lord away and I don't know where they have put Him'. In her annoyance she turned her back on the angels. She was now facing the other way, ESTRAPHE EIS TA OPISO, says John, 'she turned round'. Now she saw Jesus, but thought He was the gardener. 'Sir,' she said, 'if you have carried

Him away, tell me where you have put Him, and I will get Him.' Once again she turned her back in annoyance. Jesus spoke her name: 'Mary'. She swung round (STRAPHEISA) with the wild cry 'Rabboni'. The deepest sorrow was transformed in a moment to radiant joy!

What followed has given rise to much speculation. According to our Greek text Jesus said ME MOU HAPTOU, which could be translated 'Don't touch me' or 'Do not hold on to me', or 'Don't cling to me'. A very foolish man in a very foolish television programme said that Mary was in love with Jesus and He repulsed her, saying 'Go away, I don't want you'. There is probably no limit to the stupidity of television producers! When we examine the texts we find Ms. B has ME HAPTOU MOU and two cursives (47^{ev} and d^{SCR}) omit MOU altogether. This is pointed out by Archbishop Bernard[7] in his commentary, and he shows that if the text had been originally ME PTOOU, an easy corruption would have been ME HAPTOU and then MOU would naturally be added. It therefore seems most likely that what Jesus said was not 'Don't touch me', but 'Don't be frightened!' We all have a deep fear of anything to do with the dead, and it is easy to understand that Mary's first rapture of joy would have turned to terror when she realised that Jesus had come back to life. He therefore calms her fears and tells her that He is not a ghost! This is the meaning of 'I have not yet returned to the Father'. The verb ANABAINEIN is a rather vague word which does not necessarily mean 'to go up'. The Lord is telling Mary that His earthly ministry is not yet complete and He has a message for her to take to the disciples. There can be no doubt that Mary understood, for she went at once to the disciples with the words 'I have seen the lord', HEORAKA TON KURION, and told them the wonderful story!

St John's account of this first resurrection appearance, with its series of short clauses, does not seem like a Greek original, there is a Semitic arrangement in it which is best explained if Mary Magdalene told her story breathlessly to John and the whole episode in Mary's words, was imprinted indelibly in his mind. When he wrote his Gospel, years later, he told the story as he remembered it, and Mary's excited Aramaic could be seen in John's sober Greek.

References

1. *New Testament Christianity*. p. 12.

2. *De Incarnatione* XXX.

3. *Easter in Durham*. p. 25.

4. *Hebrew Religion: Its Origin and Development*. p. 328.

5. *Church Dogmatics* I.1.2. 114.

6. *Easter Enigma*. p. 78.

7. S. John Vol. II p. 670f.

The Resurrection Appearances of Our Lord (Lecture 2)

The second Resurrection appearance was the appearance to the women who were returning from the tomb on Easter morning. The question arises, where were they going? They may have been going to the house of 'Mary the mother of John Mark'. This was probably the house where the Last Supper had been held. We know from Acts 12[12] that it was subsequently a meeting place of the Christians in Jerusalem and it was certainly a large house. The disciples had fled when Jesus was arrested. John Wenham thinks their natural place of retreat would have been Bethany, but Peter and John followed the arresting party into the city and all the eleven disciples, with the exception of Thomas, were together in Jerusalem on the Sunday evening. But the women might have gone to St John's house, for we know that John had a house in the city to which he took the Blessed Virgin Mary on the afternoon of Good Friday. Peter and John were together on Easter morning so it is likely that they were staying in this house. Wherever the women were going, the appearance took place either in or just outside the city. Matthew says 'Suddenly Jesus met them with the greeting "CHAIRETE" (SHALOM or SHALAMA). Matthew 28[9] says 'They came to Him, clasped His feet and worshipped Him'. Their action in prostrating themselves recalls the Old Testament theophanies as in Joshua 5[14] and Judges 13[20], but the desire to touch Him showed the natural instinct to make sure that it really was Jesus, as well as a loving act of adoration.

Jesus said to them 'Do not be afraid; go and tell my brothers to go to Galilee, there they will see me.' We notice that the women were told to take a special message to the disciples, and to understand this we must refer to Matthew 26[31/32]. On the night of the Arrest, Jesus had claimed that He was fulfilling the prophecy of Zechariah 13[7] which speaks of the smiting of the shepherd and the scattering of the sheep, a prophecy which probably had no meaning for the disciples at that time. Jesus had said, however, 'After I have risen from the dead I will go ahead of you into Galilee.' H. Latham pointed out that the climax of the training of the disciples was reached in the Great Forty Days, and he suggested that the purpose of Jesus in reassembling His scattered flock in Galilee was that they might be reminded of the scenes where they had 'left all and followed Him'. We know that the disciples remained in Jerusalem for a week before going to Galilee and we must infer that this was in accordance with a subsequent instruction. We may conclude that the second appearance had the special purpose of preparing the disciples for their new commissioning for their task of evangelism.

The third appearance was a private appearance to Peter and we know nothing about it except for the references: 1 Corinthians, 15^{5}: 'He appeared to Peter' (OPHTHE KEPHA) and Luke 24^{34}: 'It is true! The Lord has risen and has appeared to Simon.' It is significant that according to St Mark, the message of the angel to the women was 'Go, tell His disciples and Peter.' Peter must have been in the depths of shame and despair and even the joyful news of the resurrection could not have brought him out of his misery. The only hope for Peter was a personal meeting with the Lord, and we are entitled to assume that this meeting was granted and Peter was forgiven his sin in denying Jesus and was restored to fellowship. This meeting prepared the way for the fuller restoration and re-appointment of Peter as an apostle which was to take place by the Sea of Galilee. Before we leave this appearance we should notice Luke 24^{12}, which says 'Peter, however, got up and ran to the tomb. Bending over, he saw the strips of linen (OTHONIA) lying by themselves (MONA), and he went away, wondering to himself what had happened.' Dr Leon Morris[1] says 'RSV and other authorities omit this verse presumably because it is difficult to see why anyone would leave it out if original.' He adds 'The words are read by almost all our best authorities for the text, the Codex BEZAE and other representatives of the Western text being the only notable exceptions. Luke tells us, as John does not, that Peter went off wondering what had happened. In view of such difficulties it is hard to think that this verse derives from John. And if it does not, then in view of its overwhelming attestation it should be accepted.' The inference is that Peter ran to the tomb a second time, this time alone, after hearing what the women had to say. But in spite of seeing the grave clothes a second time, he did not yet believe in the resurrection, for he went away 'wondering at what had happened.' By this time he knew that something wonderful had happened, but it was the actual appearance to him of the risen Lord which made everything clear. It was to a mind illuminated by knowledge of the resurrection that Jesus gave the grace of forgiveness. Here we find a very important principle: the first stage in our knowledge of God consists in acceptance of the saving facts about Jesus as they are presented to us in the Bible. When we have received and assimilated the fact of the resurrection, we are in a position to go further and to place our faith in Jesus in the New Testament sense. We come to Him, the Risen One, and receive the grace of his forgiveness. We know Him by faith and we are reconciled to God by Him and through Him: 'Ransomed, healed, restored, forgiven, evermore His praises sing.'

It was on the afternoon of the Easter day, as Cleophas and another disciple were walking to Emmaus, that the fourth appearance took place. We are not sure where Emmaus was, but the village of El Kubeibeh, which is about seven miles from Jerusalem, is a likely site. Today there is a beautiful modern Franciscan church, standing on the ruins of a crusader church. Cleophas and his friend were talking earnestly as they walked, when a stranger joined them. The phrase EGGISAS SUNEPOREUETO means that He overtook them and asked them what they were talking about. The NIV says 'They stood still, their faces downcast.' To the question, 'Are you only a visitor to Jerusalem and do not know the things that have happened there in these days?' the Stranger replied 'What things?' Karl Barth has an interesting comment at this point. He says the two 'were talking about the enacted life and death of Jesus as though it was a matter of past history.' When questioned 'They stood still gazing back like Lot's wife and were gloomy and sullen and sad.' What the disciples actually thought about Jesus at that moment, 'He was a prophet, powerful in word and deed before God and all the people .... but we had hoped that He was the one who was going to redeem Israel,' shows that they were still in the state of knowledge typical of the natural man. They did not know who or what Jesus was. The crucifixion seemed the end to all their hopes and even the news that the women had brought from the empty tomb did not relieve their perplexity or illuminate their darkened minds. It was when the Stranger began to open up the Scriptures to them, beginning 'with Moses and all the prophets', that their interest was aroused, and, as they said later, 'our hearts burned within us.' All this time they were enthralled by the Stranger. The NIV says 'They were kept from recognising Him,' and Dr Plummer[2] says 'There is good reason for believing that the risen Saviour had a glorified body which was not at once recognised.' When they arrived at Emmaus they invited Him in to supper: 'Stay with us, for it is nearly evening; the day is almost over.' While they were at table, the Stranger performed a characteristic action, 'He took bread, gave thanks, broke it, and began to give it to them,' the words LABON, EULOGESE, KLASAS, EPEDIDOU recalling the miracles of the feeding of the Five Thousand and the Four Thousand which brought recognition. 'Their eyes were opened and they recognised Him, and He disappeared from their sight.' Notice that the four actions of taking bread, giving thanks for it, breaking it and giving it, were the actions of Jesus at the Last Supper according to the Synoptists (Matthew 26^{16}, Mark 14^{22}, Luke 22^{19}). We may infer that they were characteristic of Jesus. They were certainly the basis of the later Eucharistic liturgies. The Emmaus story shows that Jesus was recognised through a familiar gesture. This raises the question, why did the risen Lord show Himself only to disciples, in other words, to those who already had some acquaintance with Him? Peter says, in Acts 10^{41}, 'He was not seen by all the people, but by witnesses whom God had already chosen - by us who ate and drank with Him after He rose from the dead.' There must have been a reason for this restriction of the appearances, and we can find it in one of the purposes of all the appearances, namely, to establish the identity of the risen Jesus. A mere appearance of a supernatural being, a phenomenon impossible to explain in materialistic terms, might have produced curiosity or fear, but it would not, by itself, have brought men to faith in the living Christ. It was essential that the witnesses should be sure, without any doubt, that the risen Lord was indeed the Jesus whom they had known and loved. This explains the very strong language of 1 John 1: 'That which was from the beginning, which we have heard, which we have seen with our eyes, which we have looked at and our hands have touched - this we proclaim concerning the word of life.' The original witnesses were so sure of the truth of the resurrection that they were able to convey that certainty to others who had not seen the risen Christ. Peter says, in 1 Peter 1^8, 'Though you have not seen Him, you love Him, and even though you do not see Him now, you believe in Him, and are filled with an inexpressible and glorious joy.'

Another feature of the fourth appearance, which is also prominent in the fifth, is the purpose of Jesus to make clear to the disciples that His death and resurrection were in accordance with the scriptures and therefore in accordance with the purpose of God.

‘Then He opened their minds so they could understand the Scriptures. He told them, This is what is written: The Christ will suffer and rise from the dead on the third day, and repentance and forgiveness of sins will be preached in His name to All nations, beginning at Jerusalem.’ Thus the resurrection was not a freak event, something isolated and alone in the whole revelation of God. It was the climax of the ‘mighty acts’ by which God had made known His purpose for this world. It was thus foreshadowed by such an event as the deliverance of Israel from their enemies by the parting of the sea. And just as God is thought of in the Old Testament as the God who brought Israel out of Egypt, so He is spoken of in the New Testament as the God who brought Jesus back to life. Some of the great hymns of St John of Damascus, such as ‘Come ye faithful, raise the strain of triumphant gladness,’ capture this idea. It is necessary to stress this point because many years ago a well-known unbeliever said that people today could not be expected to believe that a man cheated death! If the resurrection was simply about how ‘a man cheated death’ it would have no spiritual value. It might be of interest to members of the Society for Psychical Research, but it would be no foundation for Christian faith. The message of the resurrection is that it is the resurrection of Jesus Christ who is God Incarnate, the Word made flesh. And what happened to Him happened in accordance with the plan and purpose of God. Only when the message is presented like that will it be seen to be 'relevant', to use an overworked modern word.

The fifth appearance is described in Luke 24[33-49] and John 20[19-23]. It took place in the evening of the Easter Day when the disciples were together in a house in Jerusalem. Luke speaks of 'the Eleven' and 'them that were with them' (TOUS SUN AUTOIS) a description which may well have included the women - they are mentioned in Acts 1[14]. We notice that 'the eleven' are mentioned as a body even though, in fact, Thomas was missing. John tells us that the doors were shut 'for fear of the Jews'. The two disciples who had hurried back from Emmaus were admitted and they had hardly finished telling their story when all were aware of Jesus standing among them, with His usual greeting 'Peace', SHALAMA. Luke says 'they were startled and frightened, thinking they saw a ghost.' What was the reason for this panic? It is clear that these men and women had been under a very great strain. They had been plunged into the depths of grief and despair and then their spirits had been lifted to the heights of joy and wonder. And all this had happened very suddenly and within a short space of time. It is not surprising that their nerves gave way. Jesus quickly reassured them: 'Why are you troubled, and why do doubts arise in your minds? Look at my hands and my feet. It is I, myself. Touch me and see; a ghost does not have flesh and bones, as you see I have.' John tells us that He also showed them His side. The words 'It is I, myself', EGO EIMI AUTOS, in Aramaic ANA NA, are some of the most important in the New Testament: 'GRANDIS SERMO', says Bengel. They confirm our impression that the purpose of this appearance was to make clear the identity of the risen Jesus. And the appearance proved that the resurrection was a physical resurrection; it could not possibly mean anything else. Furthermore Jesus appeared in the body which had been scourged and crucified, and this proved, as nothing else could have done, that a mighty miracle had taken place and a mighty victory had been won over the spiritual powers of evil and over the unbelieving world. Jesus not only invited His disciples to touch Him, (the verb PSELAPHAO here which recurs in 1 John 1 'which our hands have touched', is HAI CHEIRES EPSELAPHESAN), but, to remove all doubt, He asked for food and ate it before them. We notice something else, the significance of which is likely to escape us because we are modern English people instead of being ancient Eastern people. Eating together was the basis of fellowship, and it was the intention of Jesus to bind these disciples together in a fellowship of which He was the Head. Up to this point they had been a society of friends, united with Jesus on a basis of personal loyalty and devotion. Very soon they would become something quite different, the Church, the new People of God, united to Jesus not simply on a human basis, but also on a new spiritual basis. This appearance, and all the remaining appearances, were concerned with the transition to the new relationship. The teaching which is summarised in chapters 14-16 of St John's Gospel would begin to mould their thinking as they began to realise that a tremendous future lay ahead of them. It is within this context that we should examine John 20^{21-23}. The words 'As the Father has sent me, I am sending ...', show a contrast which Bishop Westcott explained. The perfect tense of the mission of Jesus, APESTALKE, shows that this mission will be continued in the Church; the present tense of His sending of the disciples, PEMPO, indicates that the work which they do will be His work, not theirs. It is important to notice that the work of salvation, which Jesus came into the world to accomplish, was complete. He does not now continue His earthly ministry in the church, as is sometimes stated. In His risen presence and power He sends His Church into the world with a special task in which He Himself will be present while they speak in His name. Both Luke and John tell us what this special task is: the call to repentance and the offer of the forgiveness of sins. This is the mission of the whole Church and it is symbolised by the action of Jesus in breathing on the disciples with the words 'Receive the Holy Spirit. If you forgive anyone his sins, they are forgiven; if you do not forgive them, they are not forgiven.' The meaning is plain: it is Jesus Himself who forgives sins, an authority which belongs to Him as Son of Man (Mark 2^{10}). He now intends to use this authority on a world-wide scale by means of His Church, and the Holy Spirit will enable the Church to discharge this task. Thus, the giving of the Holy Spirit in John 20 is not a substitute for the endowment of the Church with the Holy Spirit on the Day of Pentecost. A special mission calls for a special power.

At this point we must try to form some kind of opinion about the nature of the resurrection body of Jesus. The risen Jesus could appear and disappear, pass through locked doors and appear first in one place and then in another. At the same time He could reveal Himself in a human body which could be recognised and touched and which showed the marks of the Passion. How can we understand this phenomenon? We may say that it is simply beyond our understanding, and leave the matter there. But if we do so we shall have nothing to say to those many objectors who say that the resurrection appearances were visions and that the physical appearance of Jesus was simply the elaboration of a purely spiritual experience. It is therefore necessary to examine the idea of a resurrection body which can enable us to interpret the Scriptural narratives.

In the first place, we must understand what was involved in the Incarnation. The Son of God entered our humanity by uniting human nature to His divine nature. 'The Word became flesh and made His dwelling among us.' His incarnation was not a temporary manifestation like a Hindu avatar, nor was it an occasional event, like a supposed visit of a being from outer space. He was, in fact, 'conceived by the Holy Ghost and born of the Virgin Mary.' In the technical language of theology, the manhood of Jesus was an 'addition' which He 'took'. This, of course, involved a limitation in His divine activity. St Paul expresses this in Philippians $2^{5\text{-}11}$, in which he says of Jesus, 'who, being in the very nature God, did not consider equality with God something to be grasped, but made Himself nothing, taking the very nature of a servant.' The words 'made Himself nothing' are HEAUTON EKENOSE which mean, literally, 'He emptied Himself.' A lot of study has been devoted to the implications of that phrase, but perhaps the best interpretation is that of Cyrial of Alexandria who says that it means that Jesus 'lowered Himself within the measures of manhood.'* All through His earthly life Jesus was limited by the conditions of His humanity and by the ordinary situations of space and time and matter. His miracles did not involve the suspension of natural laws, as is so often asserted, but the application of His divine power to particular earthly needs. This, we may say, was what Jesus submitted to in order that His work 'for us men and for our salvation' might be accomplished. When, however, this work had been completed and He had risen from the dead, He was no longer under any limitation. He was still man, for He did not cease to be man when His work was finished, but His manhood was now glorified, that is it was completely at the disposal of His divine nature. The atoms which had constituted His earthly body were entirely at His disposal: He could use them and reassemble them in any way He wished. Matter was now, in His case, entirely at the disposal of spirit, just as it was when God created the universe. We can go further and say that because Jesus was God incarnate, the absolute creative power of God, which had been revealed partially in such miracles as the Feeding of the Five Thousand, or the turning of the water into wine, was now completely manifested.

We can form an idea of the nature of the resurrection body of Jesus by studying St Paul's doctrine of the resurrection body of the Christian in 1 Corinthians 15. In verse 50 he says 'Flesh and blood cannot inherit the Kingdom of God, nor does the perishable inherit the imperishable.' Our present bodies are entirely adapted to the earthly life of time and space and matter. Our destiny is to receive a new body but one which will be sufficiently related to our earthly body as to preserve our identity. We shall be the same persons that we have always been but we shall be 'changed' (ALLAGESOMETHA). The connection between the two bodies is explained by the analogy of sowing a seed. Thus, 'the body that is sown is perishable, it is raised imperishable; it is sown in dishonour, it is raised in glory; it is sown in weakness, it is raised in power; it is sown a natural body, it is raised a spiritual body.' The last comparison is between a SOMA PSUCHIKON, that is a body dominated by PSUCHE, or natural life, and a SOMA PNEUMATIKON, a body dominated by PNEUMA, spirit. The comparison is then made between our resurrection and that of Jesus: 'The first man was of the dust of the earth, the second Man from heaven. As was the earthly man; so are those who are of the earth; and as is the man from heaven, so also are those who are of heaven. And just as we have borne the likeness of the earthly man, so shall we bear the likeness of the Man from heaven.' Paul thinks of Adam as typical of the human race, and Jesus as typical of the new, redeemed humanity.

It is not our purpose to enter into a discussion of New Testament eschatology, but merely to use 1 Corinthians 15 as a guide to our thinking about the resurrection body of Jesus. There is the word TAGMA in verse 23 which the NIV translates 'turn', - 'each in his own turn,' for 'as in Adam all die, so in Christ all will be made alive.' The characteristic of Jesus as a person was life. 'In Him was life,' as St John says, and therefore we can say with confidence that His resurrection was the setting free of life in its highest and fullest possible form. Theologians have followed up the clue of sowing and reaping in St Paul in their speculations regarding the resurrection body of the believer. Thus Calvin follows Augustine in distinguishing a continuity of substance in the earthly and spiritual bodies and a difference of quality. The soul is the source of the present life of the body, but the Holy Spirit, given by the risen Christ will be the source of the life of the resurrection body. Calvin says 'To make it quite clear, let the present quality of the body be called "animation" and its future quality "inspiration". For as far as the soul's giving of life to the body now is concerned, that involves the intervention of many aids; for we need drink, food, clothing, sleep and other things like them. That proves to us beyond the shadow of a doubt how frail a thing "animation" is. But the power of the Spirit for giving life will be much fuller and for that reason independent of necessities of that sort.' A modern Christian writer, thinking in scientific terms, Dr John Polkinghorne[3], has written 'For those of us who believe in the resurrection of the body there is the hope of a destiny beyond death in which the information-bearing pattern (which is the persisting element of ourselves continuing through the ceaseless changes in the matter making up our bodies) will be recreated in an unimaginable environment of God's choosing.'

All this would be mere speculation and wishful thinking unless we could be sure that at the very centre of reality, in indissoluble union with God, there is One who is alive for evermore, who is King of kings and Lord of lords, who is our advocate with the Father, who is our High Priest in heaven itself, whom we can call our Saviour. It is His resurrection which throws a flood of light on life here and hereafter. And His resurrection appearances guarantee that He is the eternal source of life and the source of eternal life. It is from this point of view that we must think about the appearance of Jesus on the evening of the Sunday after Easter Day. The apostle Thomas, who had been absent on the previous Sunday was with them on this occasion. To the strong affirmation of the disciples 'We have seen the Lord,' HEORAKAMEN TON KURION, he had replied that he would not believe unless he could see the wounds of the Passion and satisfy himself by actually touching the risen body of Jesus. Now Jesus appeared again with His usual greeting 'Peace be with you.' At once He said to Thomas 'Put your finger here; see my hands; reach out your hand and put it into my side. Stop doubting and believe.' Thomas could only gasp 'My Lord and my God.' Jesus said to him, 'Because you have seen me, you have believed; blessed are those who have not seen and have yet believed.' Thomas seems to have been a pessimist. In John 11^{16} we read that when Jesus was going on a dangerous journey to Bethany, it was Thomas who said 'Let us also go that we may die with Him.' And in John 14^{9} we have the puzzled cry of Thomas, 'Lord we don't know where you are going, so how can we know the way?' The benediction on Thomas in John 20[29] is significant. 'Because you have seen me, you have believed' uses the perfect tense, HEORAKAS, PEPISTEUKAS, conveying the meaning 'You have been given the evidence you have asked for.' Then follow two aorists, 'Blessed are those who have not seen (IDONTES) and yet have believed,' (PISTEUSANTES). The blessing is extended to all those who, in spite of the fact that they would not see the Lord in His resurrection appearances would nevertheless believe. It is a blessing for the Church in all the Christian ages.

There is a tendency today to undervalue the four Gospels because they are thought to have been written to support faith in the living Christ. A recent writer has said 'A major reason advanced for detaching faith from history is the evident fact that the documents which record the life, death and resurrection of Jesus are highly interpreted accounts. The Gospels are written from the perspective of the belief of the early Christian Community, and the stories and words of Jesus have been shaped to make a particular point in preaching about Christ.' What these modern objectors overlook is that the whole of the New Testament is radiant with the joyful certainty that Jesus Christ has conquered death and is alive for ever. To say that the Gospels are biased because they simply reflect the views of the early Church is rather like saying that Canterbury Cathedral was built because certain men had an interest in architecture. It was faith in the living Christ which, among many other things, caused great cathedrals to be built - and the faith of some modern theologians would not build a dog kennel! What we find in the Gospels, and in the rest of the New Testament, is a burning faith that has changed human lives. It has brought people from darkness to light, from death to life, from blindness to sight, from being far off to being at home in the father's house, from being aliens and foreigners to being citizens of the kingdom of God, from being a 'no people', a nothing, to being members of the People of God. This mighty change rests upon the fact that Jesus is alive, and this conviction rests upon the resurrection appearances. And Christian worship has been, from the beginning, a meeting with the living Christ. When Christians met around the Lord's Table they did not hold a memorial service in memory of a Jesus of the past. They looked back with joy to the one perfect sacrifice of the cross and the mighty victory of the resurrection. They looked forward to the Second Coming and the final victory of God in Christ. But the heart of their worship was Holy Communion, a personal reception of the living Christ who was among them and to whom they, as the Church, were united. To see the expression of that faith we need only to turn to the Epistle to the Ephesians where St Paul prays for his converts: he speaks of the 'incomparable great power' of God for us who believe, and he continues, 'That power is like the working of His mighty strength, which He exerted in Christ when He raised Him from the dead and seated Him at His right hand in the heavenly realms, far above all rule and authority, power and dominion, and every title that can be given, not only in the present age but also in the one to come. And God placed all things under His feet and appointed Him to be head over everything for the Church, which is His body, the fulness of Him who fills everything in every way.' This is our faith, and the modern secular world has nothing whatever to compare with it.

References

1. Tyndale New Testament Commentaries.
   p. 366.

2. St. Luke. International Critical Commentaries.
   p. 552.

3. Hockerill Lecture.

The Resurrection Appearances of Our Lord (Lecture 3)

The disciples of Jesus spent the first week after Easter Day in Jerusalem and then made their way to Galilee in accordance with the Lord's command (Matthew 28^{16}). In this context 'The disciples' means the eleven, for there were many disciples of Jesus both in Jerusalem and Galilee, so we must distinguish the Eleven by the title Apostles, which now comes into prominence. At some stage after the forty day period the number was made up to twelve by the addition of Matthias, Acts $1^{21\text{-}26}$, and this passage shows what was required of an apostle: 'It is necessary to choose one of the men who have been with us the whole time the Lord Jesus went in and out among us, beginning from John's baptism to the time when Jesus was taken up from us. For one of these must become a witness with us of His resurrection.'

The word APOSTOLOS is formed from the verb APOSTELLEIN which may be translated 'to send for a special purpose'. J. B. Phillips's rendering of 'Special Messenger' for apostle is therefore accurate. Luke 6^{13} says that Jesus gave the title Himself to the twelve disciples and it is probable that He used the Greek word. Luke speaks of them as apostles in 9^{10}; 17^{5}; 22^{14}; 24^{10}. Mark, in 3^{14} says Jesus chose the twelve 'that they might be with Him and that He might send them out to preach and to have authority to drive out demons.' This passage has the verb, and, according to support from uncial manuscripts, the noun as well. To sum up, then, an apostle was a man chosen by Jesus to be with Him in His earthly ministry, to be a witness to His resurrection and to be sent out with authority to preach and to exorcise. At the risk of being wearisome we must emphasise once again that the purpose of the Resurrection Appearances was not only to confirm the fact that Jesus was alive but that in His risen form He was identical with Jesus, the Man who had been known. An Apostle was not simply a witness of an event which could not be explained in normal terms; he was a witness to the continuity of Jesus before and after the Resurrection.

We find that in the New Testament the title Apostle is also applied to Barnabas in Acts 14^{14}, Andronicus and Junias in Romans 16^{7}, and James the Lord's Brother in Galatians 1^{19}. But most importantly it is claimed by Paul in 1 Corinthians 9^{1} ('Am I not free? Am I not an apostle? Have I not seen Jesus our Lord?') and in Romans 1^{1} he describes himself as 'called to be an apostle.' In 2 Corinthians 12^{12} he refers to the signs of an apostle which had characterised his ministry at Corinth: 'The things that make an apostle - signs, wonders and miracles - were done among you with great perseverance.'

It is necessary to study the conversion of St Paul in order to understand what was involved in being an apostle. This was an event with tremendous consequences not only for Paul himself but also for the Church and the world. The late Lord Birkenhead once wrote a book called *Turning Points in History* in which he examined six great decisive events in the history of the world, and he included the conversion of St Paul among them. We must therefore interpolate the appearance of the risen Christ to Paul on the road to Damascus among the resurrection appearances. We do so for two reasons, first because Paul himself regarded it as in every way equivalent to some of the appearances which he enumerates in 1 Corinthians 15, when he adds (v. 8) 'And last of all He appeared to me also, as to one abnormally born.' Second, we are convinced that the appearance on the road to Damascus proved the truth of the Resurrection as far as Paul was concerned, and had such a dramatic effect upon him, changing the whole course of his life and binding him absolutely to the service of Jesus, that attempts to explain away its supernatural character are simply not adequate. Paul as a Pharisee had certainly believed that the crucifixion of Jesus had disproved the claims of His followers that He was the Messiah, for a crucified Messiah was a contradiction in terms. He naturally used his authoritative position in Judaism to do all that he could to uproot and destroy what he considered to be a dangerous and blasphemous heresy, and it was while he was on his inquisitorial journey to Damascus to arrest the Christians there that the sudden and unexpected event happened. Now we must realise, as Dr H. A. A. Kennedy pointed out, that the conversion experience meant that Paul saw Jesus in a glorified form. It was this, the actual seeing, that convinced him that the resurrection was true and that in consequence the cross, instead of being the great obstacle to the acknowledgement of Jesus as the Messiah, was somehow a demonstration of what was meant by His being the Messiah. The *theologia crucis* was later to be at the centre of his preaching: 'We preach Christ crucified: a stumbling block to Jews and foolishness to Gentiles, but to those whom God has called, both Jews and Greeks, Christ the power of God and the wisdom of God.' (1 Corinthians 1^{23}). Furthermore, the voice which addressed him by his Hebrew name, 'Saul, Saul, why do you persecute me?' had the effect of capturing him, body and soul, for Jesus, so that many years later he was to say 'For me to live is Christ,' and to describe his conversion as KATELEPHTHEN ('I was arrested').

In his defence before King Herod Agrippa II Paul declared 'So then, King Agrippa, I was not disobedient to the vision from heaven.' (Acts 26^{19}). The word for vision here is OPTASIA which certainly means an objective vision, a seeing of something that was really happening and of someone who was there, not a mere subjective vision of the imagination. Perhaps a modern parallel is the appearance of Jesus to the Sadhu Sunder Singh, which turned him from his purpose of suicide and brought him captive to Jesus. Visions have to be judged by two things, their moral and spiritual effect upon the lives of the people concerned and their relation to the revealed purpose of God. When we consider what the appearance of Jesus meant to Paul, and what a great effect it had upon the extension of the Church and upon world history, we cannot dismiss it as a freak event. It was something planned and designed by God, as the word of Jesus to Ananias of Damascus declared: 'This man is my chosen instrument to carry my name before the Gentiles and their kings and before the people of Israel. I will show him how much he must suffer for my name.'

One feature of the conversion experience was the consciousness of a bright light: 'Suddenly a light from heaven flashed around him,' (Acts 9[3]). In Acts 23[13] Paul says 'I saw a light from heaven, brighter than the sun, blazing around me and my companions.' We are reminded of the story of the shepherds on the night that Jesus was born, 'An angel of the Lord appeared to them, and the glory of the Lord shone around them,' and of Matthew's description of the angel who rolled the stone away from the tomb on Easter morning: 'His appearance was like lightning and his clothes were white as snow.' This supernatural brightness, for which there seems to be no physical explanation, reminds us of the incident in the Gospels known as the Transfiguration, which is important because it anticipates the resurrection appearances of Jesus. It is described by Matthew, Mark and Luke, and is omitted by John probably because he regarded the whole earthly life of Jesus as a manifestation of the Glory of God ('We have seen His Glory' John 1^{14}) and he did not want to emphasise one event rather than others as associated with 'glory'. Here we notice how the Transfiguration interprets a bright light by glory. In the Old Testament the Hebrew word KABOD is associated with the presence and power of God. Dr Kennedy[1] says 'In ancient Israel, God's real presence, His actual self-revelation conceived as living energy, was constantly associated with His glory' (Exodus 40^{34}, Ezekiel 1^{28}). The setting for the Transfiguration is a 'high mountain', frequently identified with Mount Hermon and traditionally with Mount Tabor. The latter is the more likely place, for Mount Hermon was too far to the North and too high (9200 feet) for a day's climbing. Mount Tabor (1700 feet) could have been climbed in one day and thither Jesus brought Peter, James and John. We must imagine them all wrapping themselves in their cloaks and lying down to sleep in some sheltered spot on the top of the mountain. During the night the three disciples awoke to see an extraordinary change in the appearance of Jesus. Luke says 'As He was praying, the appearance of His face changed, and His clothes became as bright as a flash of lightning.' Mark says 'His clothes became dazzling white, whiter than anyone in the world could bleach them,' and Matthew says 'His face shone like the sun, and His clothes became as white as the light.' The explanation is given that He was transfigured (METAMORPHOTHE), that is, His form, or outward appearance was changed. The three disciples then saw two men talking with Jesus, whom they identified as Moses and Elijah. Then a cloud overshadowed them and a voice was heard: 'This is my Son whom I love, listen to Him.' What are we to make of this?

We can say with confidence that this was an occasion when the barrier between the world of sense and matter, and the world of spirit and eternity, was lifted for a special purpose, and earth and heaven were momentarily in proximity. We can also say that Jesus was faced with the possibility of immediately entering heaven and claiming His rightful place in glory in fulfilment of Messianic prophecy such as Daniel 7^{13-14}. He was acknowledged by the Voice of God the Father and He was welcomed by the representatives of the Law and the Prophets. The symbolic cloud that descended was the outward visible sign of the presence of God. The temptation must have come to Jesus to terminate His earthly ministry and if He had done so He would have acted in accordance with one line of prophecy, that which spoke of the kingly reign in glory. What actually happened was that Jesus resisted the temptation to claim what was His Own. He came down from the mountain and went to Jerusalem to suffer and die. He set out to fulfil the prophecy of the Suffering Servant of God, and His assumption of His glorious kingship was postponed until His resurrection. The Transfiguration, the shining of His face and garments and the light that streamed from them - this was an anticipation of the resurrection body, just as the appearance of Moses and Elijah was a guarantee that the resurrection, when it happened, would not be a freak event but a mighty act of God in accordance with His revealed purpose. We notice how the Transfiguration was followed almost at once by a prediction of the Passion (Matthew 17^{23}, Mark 9^{31}, Luke 9^{44}). We also notice how it has an affinity with the appearance to St Paul and how it has influenced Paul's description of the resurrection body of the Christian in Philippians 3^{21}: 'We eagerly await a Saviour from heaven, the Lord Jesus Christ, who by the power that enables Him to bring everything under His control, will transform our lowly bodies so that they will be like His glorious body.' The significant phrase here is SUMMORPHON TO SOMATI TES DOXES AUTOU, literally, 'conformed to the body of His glory'. This gives us another clue to the understanding of the resurrection body of Jesus. It was a body constituted by the conditions and the life of heaven. It enabled Him fully to exercise His absolute power in convincing His disciples not only of His victory over death but of their union with Him.

The story of the Transfiguration also reminds us of the spiritual world where Jesus now is and from which He manifested Himself in the resurrection appearances, and which we designate by the general term heaven. The Hebrew word for Heaven is SHAMAIM, and in the Old Testament this means first, the expanse of sky where the stars are to be seen, and second the dwelling place of God. The corresponding Greek word in the New Testament is OURANOS. God is spoken of as ‘the lord, the God of heaven’ (Ezekiel 1^{1}) and the ‘Father who is in heaven’ (Matthew 5^{45}, 7^{21} etc.). Solomon prayed ‘Hear from heaven your dwelling place.’ (1 Kings 8^{30}). Jesus came from heaven to this world; He returned to heaven when His work was completed; He is in heaven now as our High Priest and King. Jesus Himself said ‘I came from the Father and entered the world; now I am leaving the world and going back to the Father’ (John 16^{28}). In Hebrews 9^{24} we read ‘For Christ did not enter a man-made sanctuary that was only a copy of the true one; He entered Heaven itself, now to appear for us in God’s presence.’ Furthermore, Jesus will come again from heaven one day, for the word of the angels to the disciples at the Ascension was ‘This same Jesus, who has been taken from you into heaven, will come back in the same way you have seen Him go into heaven.' Heaven is also the Christian's eternal home, his final destiny. Colossians 1[5] speaks of 'the hope that is stored up for you in heaven,' and 1 Peter 1[5] refers to the inheritance 'kept in heaven for you.' Notice the two perfects here, APOKEIMENEN and TETEREMENEN, signifying that the reward is sure and certain.

We must think of heaven as being in a dimension different from those which we apprehend with our senses. Heaven is beyond or outside space and time, for space and time were created by God and God must be greater than His creation. In dealing with the physical universe we use the dimensions of length, breadth, thickness and space-time, but when we think of heaven we must think in terms of a fifth dimension, that of spirit. We may define spirit as real existence in contrast to the transitory existence of all physical objects, and as complete and perfect life in contrast to the life of all the living beings of our experience. This contrast was referred to by Jesus in controversy with His opponents: 'You are from below; I am from above. You are of this world; I am not of this world.' Incidentally, this Biblical view of ultimate reality is supported by the trend of scientific study in recent years. The old materialism of the nineteenth century in which the universe was regarded in mechanistic terms as a closed system is now generally abandoned. Archbishop Ramsay[2] wrote 'The outlook of modern thought gives no encouragement to a sharp distinction between spirit and matter or to a belief in a spiritual life that can be diametrically contrasted with bodily life. Rather does it seem to encourage us to beware of setting limits to the possibility of a bodily life that is both continuous and yet utterly different.'

We should think of heaven not only as our home after death but as the unchanging background and support of our life in this present world. St Paul says 'Our citizenship is in heaven' (Philippians 3^{20}) - HEMON GAR TO POLITEUMA EN OURANOIS HUPARCHEI - which means, as Lightfoot says, that heaven is the state or constitution to which Christians belong. This is only possible because Jesus is our Saviour, the one to whom we have committed ourselves, and He reigns as King in heaven. As Hebrews 1^{3} says, 'After He had made purification for sins, He sat down at the right hand of the Majesty in heaven.' He is the one to whom all authority has been given in heaven and on earth.

To illustrate this, we should turn to the vision of the Risen Christ with which the Book of Revelation begins. The words 'I am the first and the last, I am the Living One; I was dead and behold I am alive for ever and ever! And I hold the keys of death and Hades,' are of great importance. 'First and last' (HO PROTOS KAI HO ESCHATOS); this reminds us of the saying in John 8^{58}, 'Before Abraham was born, I am,' and this in turn drives us to the revelation to Moses in Exodus 3^{14}, 'I am who I am.' God is the

God who never changes because He is perfect in every way; He cannot *become* anything, He is the One who is. It follows that we can depend on God, and faith in Old Testament terms is simply reliance upon the word of God. In his vision on the island of Patmos, St John sees the Mosaic revelation transferred to the risen Christ. All that we mean by God is now seen in Jesus - because of His resurrection. And if it is said that St John's vision was only a subjective vision, built up from his knowledge of Jesus, we reply that such a vision necessarily presupposes the resurrection appearances. It is therefore necessary, before we consider the appearances of Jesus in Galilee, to notice the vision in Revelation 1^{12} to 3^{20}, because it is a kind of composite picture, built up from the resurrection appearances in general. The Figure knocking on the door in Revelation 3^{20}, waiting to come in and eat, reminds us at once of the meal as the bond of fellowship. In Acts 10^{41} Peter speaks of the Apostolic witnesses who ate and drank with Jesus after He rose from the dead. In Acts 1^{4} we find the word SUNALIZOMENOS, which the NIV, following the Syriac, translates 'While He was eating with them.' The meetings with Jesus during the forty days included fellowship meals intended to seal the bond of fellowship.

Other features of St John's vision should be noted. Jesus is identified with the Son of Man of Daniel 7^{13-14}, a prophecy which Jesus had claimed for Himself at

His trial before the Sanhedrin. The sword coming from His mouth is the word of God as described in Hebrews 4^{12}, the eyes blazing with fire recall Ezekiel 1^{26-28}. The fulfilment of Old Testament prophecy was of supreme importance. As Archbishop Ramsay said, 'The Jews had never expected that the Messiah would suffer and die, and thus they never expected that He would rise again. They never included in their Messianic expectations the descriptions of the sufferings of the Servant of the Lord in Isaiah 53. To them there were no scriptures that foretold either the Messiah's death or the Messiah's resurrection. Nor had the idea of His resurrection entered seriously into the expectation of the disciples of Jesus (cf Mark 9^{10}). It seems that the predictions of Jesus gave them no clear conviction, and right up to Easter morning they did not think that the Scriptures in any way foretold the Resurrection. Yet, once the event had happened they leaped to the belief that in the raising of Jesus from death the Scriptures had been fulfilled, and they proclaimed the belief to their fellow Jews.' We may add that it was the resurrection appearances which brought about this revolution in thought in the minds of the disciples.

We must now return to the re-assembling of the eleven apostles in Galilee. This was entirely in accordance with the method of Jesus in His teaching and training of these men. He had called them from their homes and work, not to a monastic life of separation from the world, but to a healthy outdoor life of constant movement and change of scene. He had not harassed them with constant and excessive instruction; their role was to help Him in controlling the crowds and to listen to His teaching. They would come to Him with their questions and He would explain in detail what He had taught in parables. He was careful that they should not be overworked: 'Come with me by yourselves to a quiet place and get some rest,' He said when they had returned from a preaching mission. During the second part of the ministry He took them on long walks so that they might have more time to think and to question Him.

The whole process of teaching was to reach its climax during the Forty Days. The Eleven had experienced the tremendous shock with which the events of the Passion had so quickly overwhelmed them. This had been followed by the ecstatic joy of discovering that Jesus was alive and that He had conquered death. What they needed now was time to think and to adjust themselves to a completely new situation. So Jesus brought them together in the old familiar scenes of childhood and youth - in Galilee where they had first left their daily work in order to be with Him. Something else was needed. These men were to be the leaders of the Church, the new society, which was to come into existence on the Day of Pentecost. From Acts chapter 1 we can see that they were quite unprepared for this. We are told that they asked Him, 'Lord are you at this time going to restore the Kingdom to Israel?' They were still thinking in terms of the prophecies of a triumphant Messiah and no doubt the fact of the Resurrection had encouraged them to think that the day of final victory was at hand. They had not yet assimilated the double strand of prophecy, that the prophets had really foretold two great events, not one. The Messiah was to come first in humility, to suffer and die for the world's salvation; He would come again in glory, at a later date, to judge the world and reign as King. In between the two comings was the age of the Church, the period of history in which the Gospel was to be preached to all nations. Jesus had already told them 'This Gospel of the kingdom will be preached in the whole world as a testimony to all nations, and then the end will come.'

It is probable that the eleven apostles had at this stage no thoughts about the future. They were enjoying their time of rest and quiet in Galilee and rejoicing in the frequent meetings with Jesus. It was therefore necessary that they should think of something much bigger than life in Galilee. Luke tells us that Jesus told them 'You will be my witnesses in Jerusalem, and in all Judea and Samaria, and to the ends of the earth.' The three areas of witness, first the city of Jerusalem, then the immediate neighbourhood, and then an extension of witnessing without limit, this was the programme for the years ahead. But one dramatic appearance in Galilee was to put the mission of the Church beyond all doubt. Matthew says the Eleven went 'to the mountain where Jesus had told them to go.' He adds, 'When they saw Him, they worshipped Him, but some doubted.' It is highly probable that this appearance, which we have listed as the eighth, is identical with St Paul's statement, 'He appeared to more than five hundred of the brothers at the same time.' H. Latham[3] supposes that some of the apostles had been instructed to summon disciples from the villages around to a meeting at a certain spot in Galilee. Latham's description of this meeting is worth quoting: 'On the top of the limestone scar, which runs by the side of the Sea of Galilee, there is a tract of comparatively level land. This was unenclosed like the moors in our north country fells, and a large body of persons might there come together without its becoming known to Herod or the scribes. At the time named, the Eleven go to the appointed place, then gradually, groups of believers appearing from different quarters draw to one spot, and there they wait and watch in an earnest way. The Eleven, I conceive, stood together, perhaps a little apart. After a while, on some conspicuous point, the figure of the Lord is seen near at hand. It is felt to be He by the great mass of beholders, and even those who are not quite satisfied yield to what we may call "the corporate conviction". They throw themselves on the ground. We do not hear that they utter any words of acclaim. There was, as I conjecture, in the Master's aspect a certain something, different from the Jesus of Nazareth they had known. The Resurrection body was not, and perhaps could not be, in all respects an identical reproduction of the functioning, organic structure of the living and breathing Being. Room is left for beholders to form their own views, and for their wishes, as well as their affection, in some measure to come into play .... Our Lord, as I figure the scene, leaving the spot on which He had shown Himself to the crowd, came to the Eleven "and spake unto them". We may suppose that those who were standing by might hear, and that they might be included in the word 'you' in the closing sentence, 'Lo, I am with you, alway, even unto the end of the world.'

We might argue that Latham has exaggerated the room for doubt and that he has been over-anxious to confine the Great Commission to the apostles alone, but he has given us, in general outline, a convincing picture. We must now, however, look at the words 'Therefore go and make disciples of all nations, baptising them in the Name of the Father and of the Son and of the Holy Spirit, and teaching them to obey everything I have commanded you. And surely I am with you always, to the very end of the age.' This tremendous universal order is based on the preceding assurance 'All authority in heaven and earth has been given to me.' It is addressed to the whole Church in general and to the ministry in particular. It is the charter of the Church's existence and activity in the world. It is not surprising that it has been attacked by criticism, especially on account of the Trinitarian baptismal formula, but W. C. Allen says 'The conclusion that the formula as here recorded marks a developed and late stage of doctrinal belief and ecclesiastical practice, is unjustified.' We can all rejoice in the promise of the unending presence of the risen Christ and joyfully accept His great commission, as Christians have done, in every great revival of the Faith.

References

1. *St Paul's Doctrine of the Last Things*. p. 91.

2. *The Resurrection of Christ*. p. 113.

3. *The Risen Master*. p. 280.

The Resurrection Appearances of Our Lord (Lecture 4)

In this lecture we shall be concerned with some of the consequences for ourselves as Christians and members of the Church of the Resurrection Appearances. And first we must notice that we are dealing with a revolution in human thought. There have been times in history when man has been confronted with new possibilities and these have had the effect of new experience, an opening up of ideas and actions; something unexpected has presented itself as a new challenge. It was like this in the Age of Discoveries, when European man became aware of the vastness of the world. It was also like this in our own generation when space travel became possible and for the first time man landed on the moon - a great step for humanity. But all human achievements sink into insignificance when we contemplate the resurrection of Our Lord Jesus Christ. This is a great intervention of God in human affairs which forms the climax of the whole process of Divine revelation which began with the Call of Abraham. We have to notice the vast possibilities which have been opened up for man as a result of the Resurrection. And first we must turn again to Romans 6[9]: 'For we know that since Christ was raised from the dead, He cannot die again; death no longer has mastery over Him ... The death He died, He died to sin once for all; but the life He lives He lives to God.'

Jesus is alive and He can never die again. He died once for all, note the strong word EPHAPAX. Leon Morris[1] says 'As Christ trod the lowly path of suffering on behalf of doomed sinners He submitted to the rule of death. But that is all past. There is no more death for Him.' This means that there can be absolutely no comparison of Jesus Christ with the founders or representatives of the world's religions. He cannot be classed with Mohammed or the Buddha or Krishna or Nanak or anyone else. He is utterly and completely unique, and consequently there can be no compromise or surrender of the Christian claim that the Gospel is for all people everywhere. The fact that Jesus is alive and that death has no power over Him has given Christians a confidence which nothing else could provide. Some of the Christians at Rome who were the first to hear St Paul's Epistle to the Romans read to them would have been among the martyrs who, a few years later, were crucified and then daubed with pitch and set alight to illuminate Nero's gardens. The Resurrection Appearances were appearances of Christ the Conqueror.

The fact that Jesus 'died to sin once for all' should be linked to His word from the cross. 'It is finished.' TETELESTAI in Greek, MUSHLAM in Aramaic, means that His death is the complete sacrifice for sin which reconciles us completely to God. He is therefore the Mediator who enables us to enter with boldness (PARRESIA) into the presence of God. It was natural that St Stephen should cry 'I see heaven open and the Son of Man standing at the right hand of God,' and that with his dying breath he should exclaim 'Lord Jesus, receive my spirit.' Furthermore the 'once for all' nature of the death and resurrection of Jesus contradicts the subtle claim made by the followers of Sir James Frazer that Christianity is allied to the agricultural religions. The resurrection of Jesus is not a resurrection of nature, and comparisons of it to the recurring cycle of the year are utterly at fault. He is alive for ever and holds the keys of death and Hades. There is a great gulf fixed between the Resurrection and all forms of Baal worship, ancient and modern.

The question may be asked, if the resurrection is in every way unique and also the supreme example of God's intervention in the world, why is it that today it is ignored by many millions of people? For most people in this country Easter is simply a spring holiday, and the idea that Jesus is alive is one which never enters their consciousness. The explanation is given by St Paul in 2nd Corinthians 4[4], when he refers to the Satanic blindness which prevents people from grasping the significance of the Gospel. 'The god of this age has blinded the minds of unbelievers, so that they cannot see the light of the Gospel of the glory of Christ, who is the image of God.' Notice the almost unconscious use of the images of light and glory, for Paul's mind, as always, is returning to the appearance of Jesus which resulted in his own conversion. And he goes on to link the resurrection appearance to the first act of God in creation, 'For God who said "Let light shine out of darkness," made His light shine in our hearts to give us the light of the knowledge of God in the face of Christ.'

Compare this language with that of Romans 6[5] in the passage to which we have already referred: 'If we have been united with Him like this in His death, we will certainly also be united with Him in His Resurrection. For we know that our old self was crucified with Him so that the body of sin might be done away with, that we should no longer be slaves to sin.' Is it conceivable that anyone should write like that about someone who was dead? Behind all this exultant language is the impression made by the appearances of the risen Christ. To be a Christian is to share in a process of death and resurrection or to experience a mighty transformation which can only be compared to the act of God in creation. Not only an appearance of Christ was needed to produce this joyful confidence, but an appearance of conquest, of triumph, of supreme and unlimited power and life.

We must notice the effect of the resurrection appearances on the Christian view of life after death. Belief in a life after death is one of the oldest beliefs. As far back as we are able to penetrate into the past we find men believing in a life after death, though they have always found it difficult to say what it is that survives the death of the body and where that something goes. It is generally thought that man has a soul as well as a body and the soul goes to the place of departed souls which may be in the sky or beneath the ground or the far West or in a distant land across the sea. In the modern secularised world many people have abandoned a belief in a life after death in accordance with the saying 'you only live once'. Now if there is no life after death, all people who have lived and died are now completely extinct and this will apply to Jesus Christ as well as to everybody else.. The fact that the resurrection has taken place and that Jesus is alive contradicts modern scepticism, but it does something more; it gives coherent expression to a doctrine of immortality which ensures that God has a purpose for us which extends far beyond the narrow limits of our life on earth. The resurrection appearances throw a flood of light on the question of a future life, for the 'Blessed hope of everlasting life' which Christians hold is bound up with the resurrection of Jesus.

The Old Testament had a poor view of a future life. The best that man could hope for was a dismal existence in Sheol, 'the place of darkness' and 'the land of oblivion', as Psalm 88[12] says. The worst thing about Sheol was that it meant an end to all fellowship with God. King Hezekiah, expecting death, said 'I will not again see the Lord, the Lord in the land of the living; no longer will I look on mankind or be with those who now dwell in this world.' Eventually this belief in Sheol was replaced by a belief in the resurrection of the body; death was thought of as a sleep from which one would be awakened at the end of the age, on the last day. We find this belief expressed clearly by Martha of Bethany, the sister of Lazarus whom Jesus brought back from death to life. When Jesus said to Martha 'Your brother will rise again,' she replied 'I know he will rise again in the resurrection at the last day.' Jesus then made the very significant reply 'I am the resurrection and the life. He who believes in me will live, even though he dies; and whoever lives and believes in me will never die.' Here Jesus assures Martha that death is not a sleep but the doorway to a conscious existence in which the believer in Jesus will be with Him. At this point we recall Paul's words in Philippians 1^{23}: 'I desire to depart and be with Christ which is better by far.'

We notice that Jesus dismissed the idea that death is a sleep in His words to the dying robber on the cross. This man had said 'Jesus, remember me when you come into your kingdom,' and Jesus replied: 'I tell you the truth, today you will be with me in paradise.' Some people have drawn the conclusion from this saying that paradise is equivalent to the doctrine of purgatory as formulated by the Roman Catholic Church, but there are no grounds whatever for this identification. The word paradise is of Persian origin and emphasises the joy and happiness of a life beyond this present world of sin. The story of the dying robber is a remarkable story of faith in Jesus and of the immediate response and assurance which that faith received. But death is not a sleep; it is the doorway to the presence of the living Lord.

In thinking about the life after death Christians have drawn on two sources, the Jewish idea of a resurrected body and the Greek idea of the survival of the soul. Thus Luther found it difficult to gather from Scripture evidence for the survival of the soul as an independent entity, and he fell back on belief in death as a sleep. He himself expected to go to sleep until the Day of Judgement when God would say, 'Wake up, Dr Martin!' Calvin, on the other hand, followed St Augustine in teaching that the soul is an independent created essence, which would have a life of its own until the Day of Judgement when it would be reunited with its body. The background to this belief was Augustine's rejection of the materialism which identified the soul with the body and his acceptance of a Platonic insistence on the reality of the soul and its superiority to the body.

We must be careful not to draw an absolute distinction between our body and our soul because both body and soul are necessary to our development as persons. Christians reject the view that our destiny is to be merged into God like a drop of water falling into the ocean. God is not to be identified with the universe in a pantheistic sense and our personality is precious to God because He loves us as the heavenly Father who loves His children. Christians also reject the idea of re-incarnation for this reason: if God has designed and planned our present earthly body, we can be quite sure that He will be able to plan and design and create a heavenly body for our life in a spiritual environment. An important passage is 2 Corinthians 5[1-4]: ‘Now we know that if the earthly tent we live in is destroyed, we have a building from God, an eternal house in heaven, not built by human hands. Meanwhile we groan, longing to be clothed with our heavenly dwelling, because when we are clothed we will not be found naked. For while we are in this tent we groan and are burdened because we do not wish to be unclothed but to be clothed with our heavenly dwelling, so that what is mortal may be swallowed up by life.’

In these verses we have a mixture of metaphors. Our earthly body is a tent, a temporary dwelling; what we look for in the life to come is a house, a permanent dwelling. Our present body is a suit of clothes; when we pass through the gate of death we do not expect to be naked but to be clothed - and, in a complete combination of metaphors, to be ‘clothed with our heavenly dwelling.’ Notice the contrast between being unclothed (EKDUSASTHAI) and to be clothed upon (EPENDUSASTHAI), and the swallowing up of what is mortal (THNETON) by life. Now this reversal of mortality is to be accomplished by God who has given us the Holy Spirit as a deposit or guarantee (ARRABON) that He will not leave us in the bonds of death. How can we be so sure that this can be our destiny? The answer is to be found in the resurrection appearances, and for Paul this meant primarily the appearance on the road to Damascus. If we survey the resurrection appearances as a whole, what kind of impression do they make upon us? Perhaps the best answer was given by Bishop Westcott in his book *The Revelation of the Risen Lord*: 'Thus Christ is seen to be changed, but none the less He is also seen to be essentially the same. Nothing has been left in the grave though all has been transfigured. He is the same, so that the marks of the passion can become sensibly present to the doubting Thomas: the same, so that He can eat of the broiled fish which the disciples had prepared: the same, so that one word spoken with the old accent makes Him known to the weeping Magdalene: the same, so that above all expectation and against the evidence of death the apostles could proclaim to the world that He who suffered upon the cross had indeed redeemed Israel: the same in patience, in tenderness, in chastening reproof, in watchful sympathy, in quickening love. In each narrative the marvellous contrast is written - Christ changed and yet the same - without effort, without premeditation, without consciousness, as it appears, on the part of the Evangelists. And if we put together these two series of facts in which the contrast is presented, we shall see how they ennoble and complete our prospect of the future. It is not that Christ's soul lives on divested of the essence of the accidents of the earthly garments in which it was for a time arrayed. It is not that His body, torn and wounded, is restored, such as it was, to its former vigour and beauty. But in Him soul and body, in the indissoluble union of a perfect manhood, are seen triumphant over the last penalty of sin. In Him first the corruptible puts on incorruption, and the mortal puts on immortality, without ceasing to "be", so far as it has been, so that in Him we may learn something more of the possibilities of human life, which as far as we can observe it with our present powers, is sad and fleeting; that in Him we may lift our eyes to heaven our home and find it about us even here; that in Him we may be enabled to gain some sure confidence of fellowship with the departed; that in Him we may have our hope steadfast, unmoveable, knowing that our labour cannot be in vain.'

For an imaginative illustration of the way in which mortality is swallowed up by life we refer to a well known scene at the end of the Pilgrim's Progress. Christian and Hopeful must pass through the river of death before they can reach the Celestial City. The troubles and distresses which assail the pilgrims as they go through the waters of death represent the fears and terrors which attack the natural man in his last hour. And the triumphant passage at last to the gate of the City illustrate the victory of the Christian in union with Christ who has conquered and subdued death. The writer says 'Then I saw in my dream that Christian was in a muse a while; to whome also Hopeful added this word, "Be of good cheer, Jesus Christ maketh thee whole". And with that Christian brake out with a loud voice, "Oh I see Him again! And He tells me 'When thou passest through the waters, I will be with thee, and through the rivers, they shall not overflow thee." Then they both took courage, and the enemy was after that as still as a stone, until they were gone over. Christian therefore presently found ground to stand upon; and so it followed that the rest of the river was but shallow. Thus they got over. Now upon the bank of the river, on the other side, they saw the two shining men again who there waited for them. Wherefore being come up out of the river they saluted them saying, "We are ministering spirits, sent forth to minister for those that shall be heirs of salvation." Thus they went along towards the gate; now you must note that the City stood upon a mighty hill, but the pilgrims went up that hill with ease, because they had these two men to lead them up by the arms; also they had left their mortal garments behind them in the river. For though they went in with them yet they came out without them. Therefore they went up here with much agility and speed, though the foundation upon which the City was framed was higher than the clouds. They therefore went up through the regions of the air, sweetly talking as they went, being comforted because they safely got over the river, and had such glorious companions to attend them.'

The idea of a spiritual body is not as strange or perplexing as it appears. Our physical bodies consist of some seven million million cells all adapted to their specific purposes. They are constantly being renewed, in fact some cells are renewed every three days. Our bodies are completely renewed every seven years or so, so that we have had several bodies in the course of our lives. There is much to be said for the Thomistic and Aristotelian idea of the soul as the 'form' of the body, that which gives life, activity and shape to the cells of the body and preserves the continuity of the self through the various stages of life. J. Paterson Smythe[2] says 'The particles of my body, of brain and nerves and heart, are constantly being changed - every few years they are completely renewed. I have had a dozen new bodies, a dozen new sets of brains and hearts since I was born - I am always wearing them out - I change them when they are worn out and throw them aside like old clothes. My thoughts and feelings are ever changing, like the ripples on the sea. But I am absolutely certain that 'I' am still there - that I am the same - just as God is the same.' There is no reason in the nature of things that just as I now have a body adapted to the conditions of life in a physical environment of time and space and matter I should not have a spiritual body adapted to the conditions of life in a spiritual environment.

What appears to us as a possibility is presented as a certainty by the resurrection appearances. As Bishop Westcott says, Jesus appears with ‘soul and body in the indissoluble union of a perfect manhood.’ The environment to which His resurrection body is adapted is a spiritual one, an eternal one. It is from this base, so to speak, that He reveals Himself. And so we can say, in the words of the Epistle to the Hebrews, “Jesus Christ is the same yesterday, and today and for ever.” It is His body which indicates what we shall have in the life to come. St Paul puts the contrast between Christ and Adam. “The first man was of the dust of the earth, the second man from heaven. As was the earthly man so are those who are of the earth. And as is the man from heaven, so also are those who are of heaven. And just as we have borne the likeness of the earthly man, so shall we bear the likeness of the man from heaven.”

It might be argued that if this is so, the Christian ought to be exempt from death. Just as the earthly body of Jesus was transformed, we ought also to expect to be transformed without passing through death. This will certainly happen to Christians who are alive when the Second Coming takes place. As Paul says, ‘we will be changed.’ But there is one great difference in this respect between Jesus and ourselves. His earthly body was transformed in His resurrection because it was essential that His victory should be manifest in His body, the body that had been scourged and crucified. For us, on the other hand, death is the inevitable means of entering the spiritual world because we belong to a fallen humanity, and death, in the Bible, is linked with sin. Because Jesus was sinless, and because He is the Second Adam, the Head of the new humanity, He was under no physical necessity to die. He said 'The reason my Father loves me is that I lay down my life - only to take it up again. This command I received from my Father.' (John 10^{17-18}). Jesus did not die by crucifixion. When He had offered Himself as the perfect sacrifice for sin, and had exclaimed 'It is finished,' He 'gave up His spirit' (PAREDOKE TO PNEUMA - John 19^{30}; PATER, EIS CHEIRAS SOU PARATITHEMAI TO PNEUMA MOU - Luke 23^{46}). As a hymn of Sedulius said, 'He died without death' (*sine morte mortuus*).

Now we must consider how the resurrection appearances have clarified our ideas of heaven, and for this purpose we turn to the Epistle to the Hebrews. The writer of this book was influenced to a certain extent by one of the fundamental ideas of Platonic philosophy, in which this world of space and time is a shadow or reflection of the spiritual world. He applies this thought to the Tabernacle of the Old

Testament, which he regards as a type or shadow of heaven. He quotes Exodus 25^{40}, where Moses is told by God that the furniture of the Tabernacle must be made according to the revealed plan: ‘See that you make them according to the pattern shown you on the mountain.’ So in Hebrews 8^{2} we have a reference to Christ the High Priest who ‘serves in the sanctuary, the true Tabernacle set up by the Lord and not by man.’ In Hebrews 8^{5} the earthly Tabernacle is described as ‘a copy and shadow of what is in heaven.’ In Hebrews 9^{11} Christ is said to have gone through ‘the greater and more perfect Tabernacle that is not man-made, that is to say, not a part of this creation.’ Finally, in Hebrews 9^{24} we read ‘For Christ did not enter a man-made sanctuary that was only a copy of the true one; He entered Heaven itself, now to appear for us in God’s presence.’ So the background is provided for the great conception of Christ the High Priest: ‘Because Jesus lives for ever He has a permanent Priesthood. Therefore He is able to save completely those who come to God through Him, because He always lives to intercede for them.’ Hebrews $7^{24\text{-}25}$. The priesthood of Jesus is said to be APARABATON, which Westcott translates as ‘absolute’, and the phrase ‘to save completely’ is EIS TO PANTELES, which may be rendered ‘under all possible circumstances’. But if we ask why it is that the work of the High Priest is assigned so confidently to the living Lord Jesus, the answer must surely be that it is suggested by the resurrection appearances. If these appearances had been vague and fleeting visions as some New Testament scholars think, or if faith in the resurrection was simply the result of wishful thinking, as Don Cupitt has suggested, it would have been impossible for anyone to invent the concept of the glorious High Priest, radiant in the perfection of His manhood who has entered heaven itself, the innermost sanctuary where God dwells in His fullness, in order to intercede (ENTUGCHANEIN) for us. The full, rich picture of the Christ who has offered Himself in perfect sacrifice for the sins of the world, and on the basis of that sacrifice is able to save completely those who come to God through Him, is quite unlike anything that is to be found in any other religion or in the godless modern world. Its uniqueness arises from the fact that it depends entirely on the revelation of the living Christ in the resurrection appearances. It is hardly surprising that some Christians, under the immense pressure of a purely secular environment have turned from the Gospel to 'another Gospel' (Galatians 1[6-7]) which, like that of Paul's opponents, is 'no Gospel at all.' Of many modern theological opinions we have to say, '*Nondum considerasti quanti ponderis sit peccatum.*' (You have not yet come to understand what a serious matter sin is.) The modern emphasis on what is called 'the social Gospels', the identification of Christianity with purely secular aims of a revolutionary character, show how far some Christians have moved from the New Testament. The condemnation of these false gospels is clear from the fact that the resurrection of Jesus has no necessary part in them. These secular gospels could be preached without the resurrection; they would be just as clear and compelling if the resurrection had not taken place!! By contrast the Gospel of Jesus Christ, which is the Gospel of the Resurrection, is sufficient to meet the deepest needs of humanity because it is all about One who has conquered death and sin and has made a complete atonement once for all. The atonement, the reconciliation of man with God, is the necessary foundation for the Christian life. The union of the Christian with Christ is the consequence of the cross and resurrection. The resurrection was followed by the gift of the Holy Spirit which brought the Church, the new people of God, into existence. The resurrection appearances in the Great Forty Days are the link between Easter Day and Whit Sunday. The apostles had to face a changed situation; the old, happy relationship of Master and pupils, Master and friends, was to be succeeded by that of the Lord and the Church. We shall see in the next lecture how the apostles were slow to understand that something new was required of them. They wanted the old relationship to continue, and the resurrection appearances would have encouraged them to hope that it would continue.

One more insight into the nature of heaven is provided by the vision of the New Jerusalem with which the Book of Revelation closes. The writer is drawing on prophetic and apocalyptic imagery in order to portray a community of perfect bliss, where 'there is no more death or mourning or crying or pain,' where 'the dwelling of God is with men, and He will live with them,' where 'there is no night and no need of the sun or the moon to shine on it, for the glory of God gives it light, and the Lamb is its light.' Two features should be noted specially: the gates of the city are open so that all may enter in, but those who do enter are those whose names are written in the book of life. There is no sin in heaven but free forgiveness is offered to all who will accept it. And the perfection of the city reflects the new creation of God, for all who are in Christ are in fact those in whom a new creation has taken place. The whole imagery of light and joy, reconciliation with God and a new life produced by a new creative act is resurrection imagery. The key to the understanding of the last great vision in the book is found in the first chapter, and the One who says there 'Do not be afraid, I am the First and the Last. I am the Living One; I was dead and behold I am alive for ever and ever. And I hold the keys of death and Hades.' The worship of the redeemed, which is the focus of the life of heaven, is described in chapter five: 'Worthy is the Lamb, who was slain, to receive power and wealth and wisdom and strength and honour and glory and praise.' Once again it must be said that this magnificent imagery would have been impossible to portray without that knowledge of the Risen Christ which only the resurrection appearances could convey.

References

1. *The Epistle to the Romans*. p. 254.

2. *The Gospel of the Hereafter*. p. 31.

The Resurrection Appearances of Our Lord (Lecture 5)

We have already noticed that the apostles were very slow to understand that during the Great Forty Days they were being prepared for their future task as leaders of the Church. It was essential during this period, that they should remain together as one body, but St John shows that they were beginning to drift apart. So when we come to John 21, which introduces what we have called the seventh resurrection appearance, we find that only seven of the eleven apostles are together, and they are returning to their former occupations from which Jesus had called them so that they might be with Him all the time. In v. 3 we are told that Peter said 'I'm going out to fish', and the others said 'We'll go with you'. St John says they went out and got into the boat and 'that night they caught nothing'.

In the early morning, as they returned from their fishing tired, cold and dispirited, they saw someone standing on the shore, who called out to them 'Friends, haven't you any fish?' They answered 'No', and the stranger then told them to throw the net on the other side of the boat. St John's comment is 'When they did so, they were unable to haul the net in because of the large number of fish'. Some commentators have been in haste to discount this huge catch of fish as a miracle. It has been pointed out that it is frequently possible for someone on the shore of the Lake of Galilee to see a shoal which fishermen in a boat might not notice, but the importance of the incident was that it would immediately recall a miraculous catch of fish which is described in Luke 5^{1-11}. On that occasion so many fish were caught that the net began to break and the two boats, one belonging to Peter and Andrew and the other to James and John, were swamped. On this occasion the net was not broken, and the words of Jesus once spoken to Peter would come back with great force: ‘Don’t be afraid, from now on you will catch men.’ The unbroken net was a silent rebuke. Their job would be henceforth to catch men for Jesus, not to look back to a past which ought to be fading from their memory.

St John tells us that he was the first to realise what was happening. He said to Peter ‘It is the Lord.’ Peter quickly slipped on his working shirt (EPENDUTES, a rare word) and tied his belt around his waist and then plunged overboard and waded ashore. The others rowed the boat in, dragging the net. Jesus was standing by a charcoal fire on which a small fish was being cooked. There was also a supply of bread. He said ‘Bring some of the fish you have just caught.’ Peter, in a restless, embarrassed mood, climbed into the boat and pulled the net onto the shore. It was full of large fish, 153 in all, St John says, for the apostles automatically counted as they emptied the net. Jesus said to them ‘Come and have breakfast’, and the meal was eaten in silence as Jesus broke bread and gave it to them together with fish. Once again a fellowship meal was the sign of union and communion and the ashamed apostles felt the joy of forgiveness and reconciliation.

The story now concentrates attention on the two apostles Peter and John. Peter had been forgiven for his three denials of Jesus but he was now to be restored to a position of leadership. The Lord’s method in this, and His wonderful insight into Peter’s spiritual condition and need should be noted. ‘When they had finished eating,’ says the text, ‘Jesus said to Simon Peter, “Simon, son of John, do you truly love me more than these?”’ The question means, as Westcott points out, ‘Do you love me, more than these, your fellow-disciples love me?’ and it refers back to John 13^{37} and Matthew 26^{33} where Peter had claimed for himself supreme devotion. The verb is the strongest Greek term for ‘love’. Peter’s reply is, ‘Yes, Lord, you know that I love you,’ but he uses the weaker expression PHILO SE. Westcott’s comment is ‘St Peter in his answer affirms his personal attachment to the Lord, appealing to the Lord’s own knowledge; but his profession differs in two important points from the question proposed. He does not assume any superiority over others; and he lays claim only to the feeling of natural love (PHILO SE) of which he could be sure. He does not venture to say that he has attained to that higher love (AGAPAN) which was to be the spring of the Christian life.'

Jesus then says 'Feed my lambs'. The work of a Christian minister is that of an evangelist and a pastor. As an evangelist he is like a fisherman, bringing men, women and children to Jesus. As a pastor he must care for the spiritual needs of the people of God and in this respect he is a shepherd. Peter had already been called to be a fisher of men; he is now given the office of pastor. The question is then repeated, and Peter's answer is the same, and the Lord's charge is 'Feed my sheep'. The variation between 'Provide for the needs of my lambs' (BOSKE TA ARNIA MOU) and 'Take care of my sheep', (POIMAINE TA PROBATA MOU) is emphatic and provides a comprehensive summary of the ministry. To be a preacher of the Gospel and to care for God's people is the greatest and most important task to which any man can be called. It is not a position which a man can claim as of right, or a profession which one can enter because it seems attractive. It is a charge which can only come from the living Christ. It is something which is, and always will be, quite unintelligible to the godless secular world.

When the Lord asked Peter the question the third time 'Do you love me?' the evangelist's comment is 'Peter was hurt because Jesus asked him the third time "Do you love me?" He said, Lord you know all things, you know that I love you.' The Greek text shows Jesus using Peter's word for love, (PHILEIS) and the reply of Jesus was again 'feed my sheep' (BOSKE TA PROBATIA MOU), literally, 'look after the needs of my sheep'. The distinction between the two words for 'love' does not appear in the Syriac text and probably did not find expression in Aramaic, but the Syriac shows Peter using the word CHAKAM for 'know' in the phrase 'you know all things', and this probably means that Peter in his confusion used the word in the Galilee dialect, for this, according to Dalman was the ordinary Aramaic word in Galilee for the verb 'to know'.

Jesus went on to predict Peter's eventual martyrdom. According to tradition Peter died in the Neronian persecution of AD 64. Tertullian says he was crucified, and Origen says that he was crucified head downwards at his own request.

The rest of the story, verses 20-24, deals with the apostle John. The writer of the Gospel wants to correct a popular rumour that Jesus had said that he would survive until the Second Coming. There can be no doubt that the Second Coming was expected to take place in a short time and the infant Church had no conception of the vastness of the work of world evangelism. The Second Coming has certainly a prominent place in the teaching of the New Testament - there are over three hundred references - and the expectation has been revived in all the Christian centuries, especially in times of persecution. The word PAROUSIA which is used eighteen times in the New Testament of the future coming of the Lord is of special importance. Moulton and Milligan point out that it had acquired a technical meaning in the Greek to describe the visit of a king or an important official to a city in person, for which preparation had to be made. It follows that the special use of the word in the New Testament emphasises that Jesus will come again in person to gather His Church and to judge the world. We can therefore say that all the resurrection appearances look forward to the Second Coming in which they will find their consummation. The final resurrection appearance is yet to take place.

The appearance of Jesus as the host at a meal is anticipated in the miracle of the Feeding of the Five Thousand, which is the only miracle recorded by all four evangelists. There can be no doubt about its importance in the ministry of Jesus, for up to this point in the story Jesus is popular with the crowds and the opposition is in the background. After the Feeding of the Five Thousand, the crowds begin to turn away from Jesus and the opposition becomes more prominent. The miracle itself marked the high point of enthusiasm - 'They intended to come and make Him king by force', says John 6^{15}. Unbelievers try to explain away the miracle by the foolish suggestion that the people had concealed supplies of food which they brought out and shared with others at the right moment. Or the suggestion is made that

Jesus was really a revolutionary and that He gathered the people together 'in a desert place' in preparation for an uprising against Rome - and the attempt failed. Or it is said that the story was simply made up in order to balance the healing miracles with a suitable 'nature' miracle.

What people fall to understand is that the Feeding of the Five Thousand was a demonstration of the creative power of God. There are two things that only God can do: only He can create, and only He can bring life out of death. Creation involves the complete mastery of God over matter, and to that extent it is a key to the understanding of the resurrection of Jesus. A great miracle, which cannot be explained in natural terms, anticipated the even greater miracle of the resurrection. The purpose of the multiplication of the loaves and fishes was to provide food, the essential requirement of life. The resurrection revealed the perfect life of God in Jesus and, at the same time, the source of spiritual life for the Christian. The link between the story of the miraculous feeding and the resurrection of Jesus is the great sermon on the Bread of Life in John 6^{25-59}. The theme is eternal life as the present possession of the Christian. This life is the present possession of all who belong to Jesus. Eternal life as the gift of God is specially emphasised in the Johanine writings: 'God has given us eternal life and this life is in His Son. He who has the Son has life; and he who does not have the Son does not have life.' (1 John 5^{11}). J. H. Bernard[1] says 'In John the thought emerges that the ZOE AIONIOS of the future may begin in the present. It is already possessed by him who believes in Jesus ... It is both a present possession and a hope for the future.'

The word AIONIOS which is translated 'eternal' is an adjective corresponding to the noun AION of which the Hebrew equivalent is OLAM. C. H. Dodd[2] says 'The word OLAM, with AION as its equivalent, denotes properly a period of time of which the beginning or the end or both are out of sight, an indefinitely long rather than an infinite period.' The emphasis, then, in the word 'eternal' is on the quality of life rather than on its duration. But the question arises, why were the earliest Christians so sure that they possessed eternal life, and why did they rejoice in the fact? There can be only one answer: By His resurrection Jesus had proved that He was the source of a new kind of life against which physical death had no power. And the resurrection appearances encouraged the hope that He intended to share this life with His followers. This is the final significance of the breakfast with the risen Lord beside the Lake of Galilee. Jesus was demonstrating by symbolic actions that the life of His resurrection body was available to His disciples. They would live 'in Christ', as St Paul says. Their new life would be nourished by the presence of Jesus. 'I am the Bread of Life' had become a saying with special relevance to the relationship between the Christian and his living Lord.

One other feature of the appearance on the shore of the lake should be noticed. We have already referred to the action of Jesus in taking bread, giving thanks, breaking the bread and distributing it, the actions at the Feeding of the Five Thousand and at the Supper at Emmaus. In John 21[13] there is a similar action: 'Jesus came, took the bread and gave it to them, and did the same with the fish.' Christian worship was to develop around the sacred meal, the Lord's Supper, which Jesus had instituted on the night when He was betrayed. The Lord's Supper was never a mere memorial feast, looking back with sadness to a past event which had ended with death. It was a joyful meeting with a living, present Lord, and the act of worship was meaningless and unintelligible apart from the resurrection. This sense of the living presence is reflected in the ancient liturgies, and the central act of worship may be described as an extension of the resurrection appearances.

The ninth in our list of the resurrection appearances was the appearance to St James. This James is generally designated 'The Lord's brother' to distinguish him from James the son of Zebedee and the brother of John, and James the son of Alphaeus. The appearance to James the Lord's brother is referred to by St Paul in 1 Corinthians 15[7]. This James was apparently converted by the resurrection and subsequently became a leader of the Church in Jerusalem. There is a curious reference by Jerome in his *De Viris Illustribus*, to a passage which he attributes to the lost 'Gospel according to the Hebrews'. This reads as follows;- 'But the Lord, when He had given the linen cloth to the servant of the priest, went to James and appeared to him. For James had sworn that he would not eat bread from the hour at which the Lord had drunk the cup (of death) till he should see Him rising again from those who are asleep .... Bring, the Lord says, a table, and eat bread' .... The quotation continues 'He took bread and blessed, and broke it, and gave it to James the Just, and said to him: My brother, eat thy bread, for the Son of Man is risen from those who are asleep.' What are we to make of this? Dr R. T. France does not rate it highly: 'Altogether this seems clearly to be a legendary expansion of a detail in the New Testament, and this perhaps gives us a glimpse into the character of what we might have expected to find if the whole of this 'Gospel according to the Hebrews' had been preserved.'

This James was persona grata with the Jews in Jerusalem. He was known as 'The Just', and when he was killed at the instigation of the High Priest Ananias in 62 AD he was mourned by Jews as well as Christians. But who was he? In Matthew 13^{55} we find the 'brothers' of Jesus, 'James, Joseph, Simon and Judas', and sisters are also mentioned. In John 7^{5}

it is said that 'even His own brothers did not believe in Him.' It is often assumed that the brothers and sisters referred to were children of Joseph and Mary, but there is at least one objection to this view. When Jesus was dying He commended His mother to the care of St John, whose mother was the sister of Mary the mother of Jesus. If Mary had grown-up sons, this would have been a gross insult and, for that reason, many people have favoured the Epiphanian view that the so-called brothers and sisters were children of Joseph by a previous marriage. Of course, this objection would not hold if the brothers were hostile to Jesus right up to the time of the resurrection, and were, in fact, unsympathetic to their mother. The important thing is that in Acts 1^{14} the Apostles are said to have 'all joined together in prayer, along with Mary, the mother of Jesus and with His brothers.'

We come now to the tenth and last of the resurrection appearances on the day of the Ascension. It seems that towards the end of the forty day period the Lord re-assembled the apostles in Jerusalem. According to Luke 24^{49} He had said, 'I am going to send you what my Father has promised, but stay in the city until you have been clothed with power from on high.' When the time came for the Ascension to take place, Jesus appeared to the apostles and led them out of the city - 'to the vicinity of Bethany' Luke 24^{50} - and then, according to Acts 1^{9}, 'He was taken up before their very eyes, and a cloud hid Him from their sight.' Luke 24[51] says 'While He was blessing them, He left them and was taken up into heaven.' The verbs relating to the 'going up' are EPERTHE and ANEPHERETO, and the mention of the cloud is important, for to Jews a cloud was a symbol of the immediate presence of God.

John Wenham[3] supposes that Jesus had appeared once more in the Upper Room and had led the disciples out in the early morning. 'After Jesus had appeared once more in the upper room the fleeting hour that followed must have been bathed in the bliss of love and trust, the eleven learning yet more of the wonderful purposes of God, and encouraged by the promise of miraculous powers to aid them in their preaching. As dawn began to break and the mists still lay on the ground they left the house and once more followed the fateful route which they had taken on the night of the Last Supper. Jesus led them out of the city gate, down into the Kidron Valley, past the Garden of Gethsemane, up the Mount of Olives, and finally "out as far as Bethany". "As far as", translates an unusual expression (HEOS PROS) which may perhaps be better rendered "as far as the path to Bethany".' The actual going up into the cloud was a plain indication that no more resurrection appearances were to be expected.

Some people do not like this story. A New Testament scholar questioned its veracity on the grounds that it is related only by St Luke. This would prompt us to ask how many times a story must be told before it becomes credible? But the Ascension is referred to in Mark 16^{19}, John 6^{62}, Acts 2^{34}, Romans 10^{6}, Ephesians 4^{7-10}, and it is the underlying assumption of the Epistle to the Hebrews. Then there are the people who tell us that the Ascension implies what is called a 'Three -storey universe'. The idea is that the apostles were simple men who believed that the earth was flat and that heaven was localised some distance above their heads, above the clouds, in fact. Now if the apostles had really believed this they would have been very sad when Jesus left them. They would have been overpowered by a sense of loss, and they would have returned to Jerusalem mourning and weeping. Instead we read that they returned to the city with great joy and they were continually at the Temple, praising God. There was certainly no sense of loss and the consciousness of the presence of the risen and ascended Jesus was very real. The actual going up into a cloud had been a symbolic action which the disciples, as Jews, would have understood. And the sudden appearance of 'two men dressed in white' (EN ESTHESESI LEUKAIS, a familiar description of Angels) who said 'Men of Galilee, why do you stand here looking into the sky? This same Jesus, who has been taken from you into heaven, will come back in the same way you have seen Him go into heaven,' would have assured them that the spiritual relationship of Jesus with His followers must be the permanent relationship until the Second Coming.

How did the earliest Christians think of heaven? Undoubtedly they thought of it first as the dwelling place of God and second as the eternal home of believers. St Paul in Colossians 1[5] speaks of 'the hope that is stored up for you in heaven' and St Peter in 1 Peter 1[4] refers to 'an inheritance that can never perish, spoil or fade - kept in heaven for you.' In both cases the participles are in the perfect, showing that the Christian's place in heaven is assured. Third, the idea of heaven is bound up with the idea of God's transcendence, that is, that God is greater than His creation and is not limited by it in any way. The Bible words for heaven SHAMAIM and OURANOS both originally meant 'the sky', but sky and what we call outer space are simply parts of God's creation which reveal His glory (Psalm 19). The earliest Christians were just as capable as we are of thinking of heaven as a spiritual world and of thinking of Jesus as present in heaven and at the same time as present to the believer and as present in His Church.

The importance of the Ascension is that it marks for us the end of the earthly ministry of Jesus and the beginning of the heavenly ministry which He is accomplishing now. It is sometimes said that Jesus is now carrying on in the Church the work that He began on earth, but this is a false idea. The work that Jesus did on earth was done perfectly and 'once for all'

(EPHAPAX); it can never be repeated. He Himself said in the great prayer in John 17 'I have brought You glory on earth by completing the work You gave me to do,' and the word from the cross 'It is finished' means 'It is completed'. So St Paul says in Romans 6[10] 'The death He died He died to sin once for all; but the life He lives He lives to God.'

The work that Jesus is doing now is that of King and High Priest and Head of the Church. In Hebrews 1[3] it is said that 'After He had provided purification for sins, He sat down at the right hand of the Majesty in heaven.' This is a reflection and fulfilment of Psalm 110: 'The Lord says to my Lord "Sit at my right hand until I make your enemies a footstool for your feet".' An ancient Eastern throne was more like a bench than a chair, and if a king wanted to honour a visiting king by showing him that he regarded him as an equal to himself, he would invite him to sit beside him 'at his right hand' in his throne. The throne of God is referred to, for example, in Isaiah 6[1] and Ezekiel 1[26] and Revelation 4[2]. God is described as a great king in Psalms 95-99. The Ascension means that the authority of God as King is now exercised through Jesus Christ. This also is the meaning of the saying in Matthew 28[18] 'All authority in heaven and on earth has been given to me.' Christians have always rejoiced in the assurance that their Saviour is also their King and that His authority and power are without limit because it is God's authority and power.

When Coligny was closely besieged and was called on to surrender he ordered an archer to shoot an arrow into the enemy lines with this reply 'Habemus Regem,' we have a King. The Kingdom which Jesus preached and which He presented in His own person was inward and spiritual - 'My Kingdom is not of this world,' He said to Pilate. The Kingdom which He will assume when He comes again, the throne of David, will be outward and visible. But the Kingdom in which He is King now is the whole creation of God, the total area in which God's sovereignty is manifested.

The Epistle to the Hebrews combines the concept of Jesus as King with that of High Priest. In Hebrews 10^{12} we find 'But when this Priest had offered for all time one sacrifice for sins, He sat down at the right hand of God.' Westcott says 'The virtue of Christ's work remains ever available as long as man's need exists.' The finality of a perfect offering is emphasised in chapter 9^{26}: 'But now He has appeared once for all at the end of the ages to do away with sin by the sacrifice of Himself.' He is the perfect High Priest because He has offered the perfect sacrifice of Himself.

It is in the Epistle to the Ephesians that St Paul unfolds the theme of Jesus as the Head of the Church. In 4^{7} he quotes Psalm 68^{18}: 'When You ascended on high You led captives in Your train and received gifts from men.' But he makes a significant alteration.

Instead of 'received from men' he says 'When He ascended on high, He led captives in His train and gave gifts to men.' He has changed the LXX ELABES DOMATA EN ANTHROPOIS to EDOKE DOMATA TOIS ANTHROPOIS. In place of the Old Testament picture of God as a victorious king bringing back captives and receiving tribute from his foes we have the picture of the risen and ascended Christ giving gifts of ministry 'so that the body of Christ may be built up until we all reach unity in the faith and in the knowledge of the Son of God and become mature, attaining to the whole measure of the fulness of Christ.'

We have here a very remarkable and highly developed concept of the risen Christ, but all that Paul says is simply the logical explanation of the consequences of the resurrection appearances. In 1^{10} it is said that the purpose of God is 'to bring all things in heaven and on earth together under one head, even Christ' (ANAKEPHALAIOSASTHAI TA PANTA EN TO CHRISTO). We have here a description of what has been called the Cosmic Christ. He who is Head of the Church is also Head of Creation. Paul prays for his Christian friends that they may know the hope to which God has called them. He speaks of the power which God 'exerted in Christ when He raised Him from the dead and seated Him at His right hand in the heavenly realms, far above all rule and authority, power and dominion, and every title that can be given, not only in the present age but also in the one to come. And God placed all things under His feet and appointed Him to be Head over everything for the Church, which is His body, the fulness of Him who fills everything in every way.'

In Romans 8^{17} St Paul says that to be a Christian is to share in the exaltation of Christ. 'If we are children then we are heirs - heirs of God and co-heirs with Christ.' He uses his favourite preposition SUN - SUGKLERONOMOI. This idea is taken further in Ephesians 2^{5}: 'God made us alive with Christ (SUNEZOOPOIESE) even when we were dead in transgressions.' In verse 6 we read 'And God raised us up with Christ and seated us with Him in the heavenly realms in Christ.' (The verbs are SUNEGEIRE and SUNEKATHISEN.) There are two things here of great importance, the union of the Christian with Christ in the Holy Spirit and the union of Christ with His body which is the Church. The Ascension prepared the way for the giving of the Holy Spirit when the disciples of Jesus ceased to be merely a company of friends united in their personal love and devotion to Jesus. They became something much bigger and stronger, a society brought into existence by a creative act of God and consequently a society utterly different from any other which had ever existed. The gift of the Holy Spirit, which in the Old Testament had been given only to specially chosen men for special purposes, now became the normal endowment for every believer.

In the great sermon of John 14-16 Jesus had prepared the disciples for the coming of the Holy Spirit: ‘I will ask the Father and He will give you another counsellor to be with you forever - the Spirit of Truth. The world cannot accept Him because it neither sees Him nor knows Him.’ There is a radical difference between the Church and the world. Christians have often forgotten this and the Church has tried many times to accommodate itself to the world. Furthermore the world cannot provide a substitute for the Church, for it does not possess the Holy Spirit which is given only to the followers of Jesus. And the giving of the Holy Spirit is the direct consequence of the resurrection and ascension of Jesus. It was all necessary, it had to be: ‘Unless I go away, the Counsellor will not come to you, but if I go I will send Him to you.’ The word which the NIV translates Counsellor and the AV Comforter (using ‘comfort’ in the Old English meaning of ‘to strengthen’), is the word PARAKLETOS. J. H. Bernard explains this as ‘a Divine helper called in, either as a witness (John 15^{26}), or as an advocate (16^{8}), or as an adviser (16^{13}).’

It is important to understand that the giving of the Holy Spirit on the Day of Pentecost was the climax of the resurrection appearances. The phenomena accompanying the gift, the speaking so that people of various languages could understand the message so that many were converted, was not an isolated event. Considered simply by itself, what happened on the Day of Pentecost could be classed with many kinds of spiritual experience or it could be described as just one instance of ecstatic behaviour or spiritual excitement. But it was not an event which happened in isolation from all the other events associated with the life and ministry of Jesus. And it was an event of immense influence and of tremendous consequences, for it was the birthday of the Church. To explain it, to give an intelligible account of what happened on the day we have to refer to the resurrection of Jesus and to the resurrection appearances which authenticated the fact of the resurrection. The final proof of the resurrection of Jesus Christ is the existence of the Christian Church.

References

1. St John. Vol. I. p. clx.

2. *The Interpretation of the Forth Gospel.* p. 144.

3. *Easter Enigma.* p. 121.

The Resurrection Appearances of Our Lord (Lecture 6)

In this last lecture we must try to assess the permanent significance for the Church of the New Testament stories of the resurrection appearances of Jesus. We may say that their importance first of all is evidential. They supply the proof of what the Empty Tomb implies, that Jesus rose again in His physical body in such a way that His identity was established, and, at the same time, His conquest of sin and death was made certain. There can be no doubt that the New Testament speaks of a physical resurrection. It shows us a miracle, greater than all other miracles, which it ascribes to the power of God. The conviction of the first Christians was that it was a mighty demonstration of the power of God. 'God raised Him from the dead'. (Acts 3^{15})

This clear teaching of the New Testament has been questioned by some people in recent years, notably by Bishop Jenkins.* The Bishop's views on the resurrection are summarised in a booklet entitled *Easter in Durham*, by Dr Murray J. Harris[1], and published by the Paternoster Press, Exeter. It seems that it is the physical resurrection which the Bishop rejects. He regards the resurrection as something that took place in the minds of the disciples. He says 'You cannot tell precisely what happened at the first

Easter nor get behind the experiences, encounters and discoveries of the early Church and their way of telling the stories of faith.' Dr Harris comes to this conclusion after examining the Bishop's views: 'In all his writings Bishop Jenkins has consistently argued that Jesus' resurrection was God's act of perpetuating the presence and power of Jesus among His disciples after His death. Jesus rose, not bodily, from the grave, but spiritually (although none the less really), in the minds of the disciples. The basic flaw of such a view is that it confuses the nature and the effect of the resurrection ... According to the New Testament the resurrection of Jesus was His bodily and permanent emergence from death in a transformed state, and His exaltation to God's right hand. When the empty tomb and appearances of Jesus had made it clear that He had been reanimated and transformed, faith in the risen Jesus was born in His followers. We must never lose sight of the necessary distinction between the resurrection fact and the resurrection faith .... The disciples' faith in the risen Jesus derived its validity from the prior fact that Jesus rose from the dead.'

Christianity is built on facts, not fancies, and it is a fact that in the resurrection something very big happened which changed the course of history. Now a big effect demands a big cause to account for it and no-one has yet been able to find a substitute event which could have produced the results which the New Testament attributes to the resurrection. St Luke tells us that Jesus showed that He was alive (EN POLLOIS TEKMERIOIS), which the NIV translates 'many convincing proofs', and the AV 'many infallible proofs'. St Luke uses a medical word which was used when a disease had been 'proved'. The facts made the conditions clear beyond reasonable doubt.

In the second place the resurrection appearances show Jesus not as the suffering servant of Old Testament prophecy but as the Messianic King. The sufferings of Jesus, as they are portrayed in the Gospels, were very great. He was mocked, insulted, beaten up, spat upon, crowned with thorns, scourged and crucified. The question is naturally asked, why? And the answer usually given is that He had claimed to be the Messiah in fulfilment of Daniel 7[13-14], which the Jews regarded as blasphemy and the Romans interpreted as a political claim to kingship. It is also said that the people rejected Him because He refused to be the kind of Messiah they had expected. But these explanations do not account for the furious hatred which was directed against Jesus. Now we know, only too well, how powerful and evil hatred can be in this bloodstained twentieth century. We know about the hatred of Nazis for Jews, of Communists for so-called capitalists, of the IRA for all Englishmen, and of left wing mobs for the police. But why was Jesus hated? The answer is that He identified Himself so completely with the One whom the prophets had said would be smitten and would suffer that men saw the nature and character of God revealed in Him. The loving-kindness of God (CHESED) by which the prophets had described God's persistent attitude to Israel, was suddenly set before them in a human person and a human life. Now this produced a predictable reaction, for the natural man does not want God to come too close. He has no objection if God remains in heaven, but if He comes down to earth and offers Himself to him in a form to which he can respond, that is another matter entirely. Jesus suffered because men were not only determined to get rid of Him, but also to show their rejection. 'It's our world and we do what we like with it,' is the cry of the natural man, men going their own way and living their lives without reference to God. And if the resurrection had not taken place the natural man would have taken over the world and it would have been no longer God's world. The resurrection appearances, therefore, show the triumph of God. They show God victorious in every way, over death, over matter, over the world's hatred and rejection, over doubt and despair.

Natural man is fallen man, man in need of redemption, man to whom the offer of salvation is now directed. Jesus Christ was born in order to save the world: 'God did not send His Son into the world to condemn the world, but to save the world through Him.' This work of salvation was accomplished by Jesus through His death on the cross and was made known and made available to all by His resurrection. 'He was delivered over to death, for our sins and was raised to life for our justification.' Leon Morris says of this verse 'Paul is affirming strongly that it was for our sins that Christ died and that He has perfectly accomplished our justification.' To be justified does not mean to be made righteous, but to be treated as righteous. To quote Leon Morris again, 'The word is a forensic or legal term with the meaning "acquit". It is the normal word to use when the accused is declared "Not guilty".'

The effect of the resurrection appearances was to give assurance that salvation from sin was now available through Jesus Christ. In Acts 5^{31} St Peter says 'God exalted Him to His own right hand as Prince and Saviour that He might give repentance and forgiveness of sins to Israel.' In Acts 13^{38} St Paul says 'Therefore, my brothers, I want you to know that through Jesus the forgiveness is proclaimed to you. Through Him everyone who believes is justified from everything you could not be justified from by the law of Moses.' The effect of sin in separating man from God is reversed when sin is forgiven and fellowship with God is restored. This tremendous change is the theme of worship in the New Testament: 'To Him who loves us and has freed us from our sins by His blood, and has made us to be a kingdom and priests to serve His God and Father - to Him be glory and power for ever and ever! Amen!' (Revelation 1^{5-6}).

‘Worthy is the Lamb who was slain, to receive power and wealth and wisdom and strength and honour and glory and praise’ (Revelation 5[12]). ‘For you know that it was not with perishable things such as silver and gold that you were redeemed from the empty way of life handed down to you from your forefathers, but with the precious blood of Christ, a lamb without blemish or defect’ (1 Peter 1[18-19]). This joyful conviction could never have existed without the resurrection, which confirmed the effect of the perfect sacrifice; and the triumphant character of the resurrection and all that it meant was made known by the resurrection appearances. If the disciples of Jesus had not known His risen presence, the whole experience of restoration to fellowship with God, which is utterly different from that of any other religion, would never have been known.

In a recent report in the Church Times, Bishop Montefiore said ‘The story of God incarnate in Jesus of Nazareth cannot be heard by most people today. The very idea of God incarnate is for them a myth, or a wish-fulfilling delusion, or a blown-up story of someone who was a good man; certainly not a story about the life, death and resurrection of the One who gives us a clue to the nature of God, and the meaning of the cosmos and the purpose of our existence.’ This modern attitude is a compound of ignorance and indifference; it is certainly not the result of deep study of the sources of the Christian faith in the New

Testament, and it indicates a total disregard of the resurrection. By contrast, the New Testament is built on the resurrection and it was the resurrection appearances which formed and moulded the faith which conquered the pagan world. Dr B. B. Warfield[2] wrote 'It would seem impossible, in fact, to read the New Testament and miss observing that not only to Paul, but to the whole body of the founders of Christianity, the conviction of the reality of Christ's bodily resurrection entered into the very basis of their faith. The fact is broadly spread upon the surface of the New Testament record. Our Lord Himself deliberately staked His whole claim to the credit of men upon His resurrection. When asked for a sign He pointed to this sign as His single and sufficient credential. The earliest preachers of the Gospel conceived witnessing to the resurrection of their Master to be their primary function. The lively hope and steadfast faith which sprang up in them they ascribed to its power.'

Let us notice how some of these predictions of Jesus regarding His resurrection are found in the Gospels. In John 2[18] Jesus says 'Destroy this temple and I will raise it again in three days.' The evangelist comments 'The temple He had spoken of was His body.' In Matthew 12[40], with reference to 'the sign of the prophet Jonah,' it is said 'for as Jonah was three days and three nights in the belly of a huge fish, so the Son of Man will be three days and three nights in the heart of the earth.' In Mark 8^{31} Jesus warns the disciples that 'The Son of Man must suffer many things and be killed and after three days rise again.' This prediction is repeated in Mark 9^{30} and 10^{34}. Now Hoskyns and Davey, in their commentary on St John's Gospel, point out that phrases like 'after three days' or 'on the third day' mean 'The day after tomorrow.' A guest seeking hospitality was expected to leave on the third day. To stay longer was a claim to permanent residence. It follows that when Jesus told His disciples that He would rise again 'after three days' He meant them to understand that He would be a guest in the spiritual world, not a permanent resident. The phrase in Matthew 12^{40} 'in the heart of the earth' simply means Hades or the spiritual world, as Irenaeus and Tertullian pointed out. There is a parallel to it in Ephesians 4^{9} where Jesus is said to have descended to 'the lower, earthly regions.' We have to notice that two questions have been frequently asked. 1) Why did Jesus rise on the third day? Why did the resurrection not take place on Good Friday and in such a public way as to confound His enemies? 2) What was Jesus doing in the time between His death on the cross and His showing of Himself alive on the Easter Day? The answer to the first question would seem to be that a public and dramatic act might have produced the kind of 'evidence' which is demanded by the modern unbeliever, but it would not have given rise to the kind of faith on which the

Christian life is built. It would, indeed, have been an answer to the taunt ‘Let Him now come down from the cross and we will believe in Him;’ and behind the taunt was the old temptation to demonstrate the Kingdom of God by worldly means. The resurrection took place in secret, no-one saw it happen. Moreover, the manner of the resurrection introduced a new day, the Lord’s Day (Revelation 1^{10}), the first day of the week, which was to become the sabbath of the New Covenant as a substitute for the sabbath of the Old Covenant. When we consider how important Sunday has been as the day of rest and worship and the weekly witness to the truth of the resurrection, we can understand that the godless modern world would do everything in its power to destroy its significance, and to turn it into what it has become, the weekly wasted day, the day of lost opportunity.

Jesus promised the dying terrorist that he would be with Him in Paradise on the day of his death. The only Scriptural comment on this is in 1 Peter 3^{19} & 4^{6}. The first verse reads ‘He was put to death in the body but made alive by the Spirit, through Whom also He went and preached to the spirits in prison who disobeyed long ago when God waited patiently in the days of Noah while the ark was being built.’ The second verse reads ‘For this is the reason the Gospel was preached even to those who are now dead, so that they might be judged according to men in regard to the body, but live according to God in regard to the spirit.' Much has been written about the *Descensus ad Inferos* as it is called, and we might notice the comment of Professor Bernard Weiss: 'He in the Spirit went down to the spirits in prison in order to bring the message of redemption to these also, as He had brought it to mankind on earth ..... But as this blessing of His death extends backwards to the earliest ages of mankind, it also extends forward to the end of days.'

However we interpret these verses in 1 Peter, they direct our attention to the complete and final significance of the resurrection. The fact that Jesus rose again 'on the third day' makes it clear that He had been active in the spiritual world and therefore that world is not beyond the reach of His life-giving power. Just as the Creation story of Genesis 1 shows that there is no realm of chaos in opposition to God, so the resurrection appearances are preceded by the assurance that the victorious Christ is not to be opposed or resisted by any kind of chaos or darkness or evil. In the old pagan religions the power of the high gods was always limited, either by fate or the realm of the dead. The resurrection of Jesus proves that there is no power anywhere that can resist Him.

Jesus Christ was completely human; as man He was a union of body and soul, a soul/body Person. There was a heresy in the fourth century associated with a theologian named Apollinaris which is said to have asserted that Jesus did not have a human soul, the place of it having been taken by the logos. But if Jesus went to the spiritual world when He died. He must have gone there in His soul. This means that Jesus experienced human life in His body and human death in His soul, so there was no sense in which He was not completely man. Now the substantiality of the soul is something which is always denied by materialists. Western theology owed a great debt to St Augustine. Ludger Hölsher notes 'Employing the introspective method as only very few thinkers have, Augustine gained an understanding of man's inner being that, as should have become evident, in its originality and sharpness of insight has rarely been equalled.' The Greek theologians, on the other hand, looked back to Plato for a conception of the soul as a spiritual essence, superior to the body and in its rational nature governing and directing the unruly desires of the flesh. But if we look back to Jesus as the one man in whom body and soul were in perfect adjustment and both were wholly united to God, we can begin to see the resurrection as the complete triumph of manhood as God intended it to be. In other words, just as the Son of God in becoming incarnate took human nature and united it to His divine nature, so in rising from the dead He raised human nature itself. Jesus did not cease to be man; for ever and ever He will be human as well as divine. This is the truth expressed in Article IV of the thirty nine Articles: 'Christ did truly rise again from death, and took again His body, with flesh, bones and all things appertaining to the perfection of Man's nature; wherewith He ascended into Heaven, and there sitteth, until He return to judge all men at the last day.'

Dr Bultmann poured scorn on the physical resurrection of Jesus as the re-animation of a corpse. This is something that it certainly was not. We have, however, in the Gospels three miracles of the raising of the dead which could be described as re-animation for in each case a person was brought back to natural life and, of course, subsequently died. The daughter of Jairus had only just died when Jesus called her back. The widow's son at Nain had been dead for a few hours, and Lazarus of Bethany had been dead for four days. The raising of Lazarus is of particular significance because, as St John indicates, it brought the opposition to Jesus to a head. It is sometimes objected that it cannot be regarded as historical because it is only recorded by St John, but an explanation is needed, which the Synoptics do not supply, to account for the murderous intentions of Caiaphas and the Sanhedrin. The fact that Lazarus had been dead for four days indicted, as we have already explained, that according to contemporary thought, he was a permanent resident in the realm of the dead, and a comment once made by a Christian doctor, looking at the story from a medical point of view, declared that after four days 'irreversible changes have occurred of such a kind that the restoration of life can be looked upon by those acquainted with human physiology as wholly extraordinary, and, in these circumstances, as miraculous.' We have here a miracle which illustrates the power of Jesus to give physical life, and therefore also spiritual life. It shows that the creative power of God was in Jesus, and it forms a climax to the teaching in chapter 6 regarding Jesus as the source of spiritual life and in chapter 8 as the light of life. It was a miracle in which death had to yield to the Word of God which was in Jesus.

There are several important points to notice in this story, one of them is that Jesus encountered unbelief - from the disciples, from Martha and Mary, the sisters of Lazarus, and from the friends present. We should note also the conversation between Jesus and Martha in which Jesus corrects the current view of death as a sleep. In reply to His words 'Your brother will rise again,' Martha's reply was 'I know he will rise again in the resurrection at the last day.' Jesus then said 'I am the resurrection and the life. He who believes in me will live, even though he dies; and whoever believes in me will never die.' In these few words Jesus corrected the current idea of death as a sleep and substituted for it the concept of eternal life as the life of the soul in union with Himself. Death cannot destroy this life because Jesus has conquered death. The Christian bases his hope of a life after death not on a metaphysical theory of the nature of the soul but upon the concrete fact of union with Christ.

The raising of Lazarus was, of course, the re-animation of a physical body, but the resurrection of Jesus was something quite different; it was the complete transformation of His physical body, to which His soul was re-united. Jesus is thus revealed as God and Man, His divine nature indissolubly united with His human nature, as one divine/human Person. In seeking to understand the meaning for us today of the resurrection appearances, we must notice that they lead us steadily to the formulation of belief adopted by the Council of Chalcedon in 451 AD. This stated: 'Wherefore, after the example of the holy Fathers, we all with one voice confess our Lord Jesus Christ one and the same Son, the same perfect in Godhead, the same perfect in manhood, true God and true man, the same consisting of a reasonable soul and a body, of one substance with the Father as touching the Godhead, the same as one substance with us as touching the manhood, like us in all things, sin except; begotten of the Father before all worlds as touching the Godhead, the same in these last days, for us and for our salvation, born of the Virgin Mary, the Mother of God, as touching the manhood, one and the same Christ, Son, Lord, Only-begotten, to be acknowledged in two natures, without confusion, without change, without division, without separation; the distinction of natures being in no wise done away because of the union, but rather the characteristic property of each nature being preserved, and concurring into one Person and one substance, not as if Christ were parted or divided into two Persons, but one and the same Son and Only-begotten God, Word, Lord, Jesus Christ: even as the prophets from the beginning spake concerning Him, and our Lord Jesus Christ hath instructed us, and the Symbol of the Fathers hath handed down to us.'

This is highly technical theological language, but behind it there was a long period of discussion and controversy until the full meaning of the New Testament facts was apparent. Dr B. B. Warfield[3] wrote 'The constancy with which the Church has confessed the doctrine of the two natures finds its explanation in the fact that this doctrine is entrenched in the teaching of the New Testament. The Chalcedonian Christology, indeed, in its complete development is only a perfect synthesis of the biblical data. It takes its starting point from the New Testament as a whole, thoroughly trusted in all its declarations and seeks to find a comprehensive statement of the scriptural doctrine of the Person of Christ, which will do full justice to all the elements of its representation. The eminent success which it achieves in this difficult undertaking is due to the circumstance that it is not the product of a single mind working under a "scientific" impulse, that is to say, with purely theoretical intent, but the mind, or rather the heart, of the Church at large searching for an adequate formulation of its vital faith, that is to say, of a large body of earnest men, distributed through a long stretch of time, and living under very varied conditions, each passionately asserting, and seeking to have justice accorded to, elements of the biblical representation which particularly "found" him ...' If we find the theological language puzzling, we should remember, as Bishop Stephen Neill reminded us that 'those who worked out the Christian doctrines were simply trying to express in words an inexpressible experience.' But the theological formulae are intended to guard us against certain errors. For example, we must not think of Jesus Christ as behaving sometimes as God and sometimes as man, like an actor appearing in two different roles. Whatever He did, He did as both God and man; in Him Godhead and manhood were indissolubly united in one perfect Person.

This is illustrated, for example, by the appearance of Jesus to the disciples on the evening of Easter day. He appears, suddenly, when the doors of the room were shut, and quiets their fears by showing them His hands and feet and side. He invites them to touch Him and eats before them. He also claims that the Scriptures have been fulfilled by His death and resurrection and He commissions them to preach forgiveness of sins in His Name. Here Docetism is rebuked - the theory that Jesus only seemed to be human. Here modern secularism is rebuked - the refusal to accept Jesus as God incarnate. But Jesus is showing Himself as a complete Divine and human Person.

The Christology of the New Testament, its teaching regarding the nature of Christ, is built on the resurrection as its foundation. We may distinguish (1) **The contribution of St Paul**. Here Jesus is described as the Son of God: Romans 1^{4}; 5^{10}; 1 Corinthians 1^{9}; Galatians 4^{4}. This suggests a unique relationship with God. In Romans 3^{24} it is said that God presented Him as a sacrifice of atonement (HILASTERION) through faith in His blood. In Romans 5^{12-21} Jesus is described as the second Adam in whom the human race has a new beginning, and in 2 Corinthians 5^{21} we find an anticipation of what later theology would call the Glorious Exchange, 'God made Him who had no sin to be sin for us, that in Him we might become the righteousness of God.' In Colossians 1^{15-20} there is a summary of the work of what might be called the Cosmic Christ. He is the image of the invisible God, the first-born over all creation. By Him all things were created (DI'AUTOU KAI EIS AUTON, 'by Him and for Him'). Moreover, 'He is before all things and in Him all things hold together.' He is also the Head of the Church and 'the first-born from among the dead (HE ARCHE, PROTOTOKOS EK TON NEKRON) so that in everything He might have the supremacy.' The exalted position of Christ is related to the resurrection in Ephesians 1^{19-23}. Paul refers to 'His incomparable great love for us who believe.' (TO HUPERBALLON MEGETHOS TES DUNAMEOS.) 'That love is like the working of His mighty strength, which He exerted in Christ when He raised Him from the dead and seated Him at His right hand in the heavenly realms.' The conclusion is, 'And God placed all things under His feet and appointed Him to be head over everything for the Church, which is His body, the fullness of Him who fills everything in every way.'

(2) **The Interpretation of St John**. The fourth Gospel begins 'In the beginning was the Word.' The Greek word 'logos' translated 'word' means not only the spoken word but the thought or reason of which it is the expression. It corresponds to the Aramaic word MEMRA which is used in the Targums as a synonym for God as it means the expression in personal form of the Word. It recalls the Hebrew DABAR which is the Word of Command by which God created the universe. St John reminds us that God had no beginning and yet He has never been alone; He has expressed Himself fully in His Word by whom He created all things and who is the source of life. It is He who became flesh and made His dwelling among us, and we have seen His glory. Notice the appeal to personal testimony, a feature also of the First Epistle of St John. Then the incarnation of the Word is spoken of in personal terms. He is Jesus the Christ,

the Anointed One, the King of Old Testament prophecy. Jesus claims the unique relationship with God expressed by the title Son: 'I tell you the truth, the Son can do nothing by Himself; He can only do what He sees the Father doing, because whatever the Father does the Son does also.' In this connection we notice the great 'I am' sayings: 'I am the Bread of Life, the Light of the World, the Good Shepherd, the Door of the Fold, the Way, the Truth and the Life, the Resurrection and the Life, the True Vine.' These claims are reinforced by the sayings 'Before Abraham was, I am' and 'I and the Father are One.' Jesus claims identity with God and the sacred Name 'I am' of the revelation to Moses in Exodus 3: 'I am that I am.' These tremendous claims would be either meaningless or blasphemous unless they rested upon the mighty demonstration of the Resurrection. If anyone doubts the physical nature of the resurrection we are entitled to ask whether a work of genius such as St John's Gospel could ever have been written without personal knowledge of the risen Christ. Dr Marcus Dods said of the Fourth Gospel: 'In the whole range of literature there is no composition which is a more perfect work of art, or which more rigidly excludes whatever does not subserve its main end. From the first word to the last there is no paragraph, sentence or expression which is out of its place, or with which we could dispense. Part hangs together with part in perfect balance .... The object which the

Evangelist had in view in writing this Gospel we are not left to find our for ourselves. He explicitly says that his purpose in writing was to promote the belief that "Jesus is the Christ, the Son of God".'

(3) **The Christology of the Epistle to the Hebrews**. 'In point of time' says Dr H. R. Mackintosh[4], 'the Epistle to the Hebrews is the first systematic sketch of Christian theology. A very complete picture of Christ is drawn, line after line being added to fill out the majestic introductory representation (1^{1-14}).' Jesus is our great High Priest. The author argues that although Jesus was not of Aaronic descent, His High Priesthood is better than that of the Levitical priests for it was of the order of Melchizedek, being the fulfilment of Psalm 110^{4}. Moreover His priesthood rests, as 7^{16} says, 'on the basis of the power of an indestructible life.' Westcott says 'The life of Christ was not endless or eternal only. It was essentially "indissoluble" (AKATALUTOS).' He adds 'It must be further noticed that the possession of this indissoluble life is not only characteristic of Christ's exercise of His priestly office: it is the ground on which He entered upon it. Other priests were made priests in virtue of a special ordinance: He was made priest by virtue of His inherent nature. He could be, as none other, victim at once and priest.'

The Epistle to the Hebrews emphasises the resurrection as firmly as it does the sacrifice of the

Cross. In 10^{10} we read 'we have been made holy through the sacrifice of the body of Jesus Christ once for all.' (EPHAPAX.) In 7^{24} 'Because Jesus lives for ever, He has a permanent priesthood' (APARABATON, which Westcott renders 'absolute'). The conclusion is then drawn, 'Therefore He is able to save completely those who come to God through Him, because He always lives to intercede for them.'

We have seen that the New Testament presupposes the resurrection of Jesus Christ and is utterly unintelligible without it. But the resurrection in itself would have remained a vague idea unless it had been given visual expression by the Resurrection Appearances. The proof of the truth of the fact of the Resurrection, demonstrated by the appearances, is the Faith itself, a faith sealed not only by the blood of many martyrs, but by the changed lives of a vast number of men and women who with one voice would testify that He has 'brought us from darkness to light and from the power of Satan to God.' That Faith exists today and, wherever the Gospel is preached in the power of the Spirit, the 'power of His Resurrection' is as effective today as ever it has been in the past, and we can be sure it will continue to be until the Lord's Coming Again.

References

1. *Easter in Durham.* p. 31.

2. *The Person and Work of Christ.* p. 537.

3. *Ibid.* p. 215.

4. *The Person of Jesus Christ.* p. 78.